Praise for Stubborn Life

"Rarely do people write about such great tragedies as calmly as Michalska does—without complaint, without blame. The dispassionate style of the narrative strengthens the impact of the description. This is a story about the will to survive, and about the joy that comes from that survival. Awe-inspiring—I read this incredible recollection in one breath."
Granice

"A sober hymn to tenacity and courage. This determined woman tells her story in a neutral tone, without pathos, without bitterness, without incriminating or nationalist reproaches. Despite everything, solidarity, dedication, and kindness persist."
Les Notes

"What a story! *Stubborn Life* is both a glimpse into all the complexities and cruelties of the Soviet twentieth century, and a sober and powerful account of a life marked as much by the determination to move forward as by 'the memory of all those (...) who stayed there forever.'"
Passage à l'Est

Stubborn Life

FRANCESKA MICHALSKA

Stubborn Life

Hardship and Hope in
Ukraine, Kazakhstan, Poland

Translated from the Polish
by Sean Gasper Bye

WORLD EDITIONS
New York

Published in the USA in 2023 by World Editions NY LLC, New York

World Editions
New York

English translation copyright © Sean Gasper Bye, 2023
The book uses photographs from the author's archive and
three photographs from the period of great famine in
Ukraine in 1932–1935 © ITAR TASS/SIPA
Author portrait © Agencja Gazeta

Printed by Lightning Source, USA

Background image by Dan Cristian Pădureț via Unsplash

Library of Congress Cataloging in Publication Data is available

ISBN 978-1-64286-152-5

First published as *Cała radość życia* in Poland in 2007
by Oficyna literacka Noir sur Blanc, Warszawa

This book has been published with the support
of the ©POLAND Translation Program

Company: worldeditions.org
Facebook: @WorldEditionsInternationalPublishing
Instagram: @WorldEdBooks
TikTok: @worldeditions_tok
Twitter: @WorldEdBooks
YouTube: World Editions

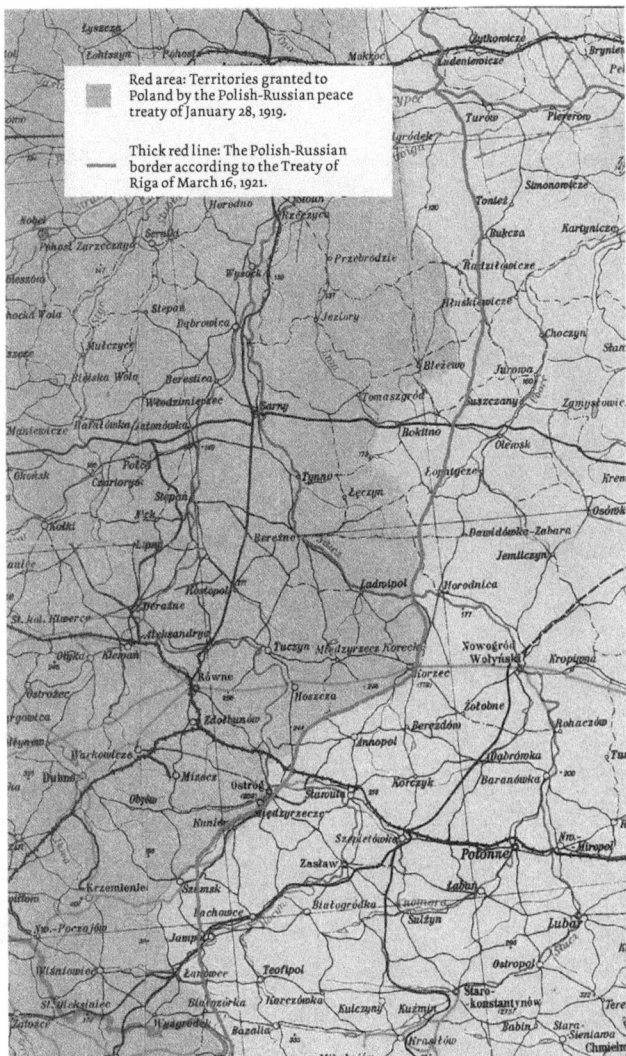

Red area: Territories granted to Poland by the Polish-Russian peace treaty of January 28, 1919.

Thick red line: The Polish-Russian border according to the Treaty of Riga of March 16, 1921.

VOLHYNIA

A map of the author's home region.

Midway between Berezdiv and Slavuta lies the village of Marachivka.[1] In the days of the tsar, the guberniya administration there was in Shepetivka. After the revolution, the area fell within Vinnytsia Oblast, and Slavuta was made the seat of a raion. Later, Vinnytsia Oblast was split and a new okrug was created, containing Shepetivka, Slavuta, and Berezdiv. After the First World War, the Polish-Bolshevik War, and finally after the Treaty of Riga between Poland and Soviet Russia, these lands remained on the Soviet side. The nearest city on the

---

1   See the translator's note on place names.

Polish side was Korets, which was twenty-five kilometers from Berezdiv. Every year on June 13, the Feast of St. Anthony, the local people had the custom of traveling to Korets, to the church under his patronage there. The custom survived for a little while after the new border was set. These excursions required bribing the Soviet border guards. The soldiers appeared very impoverished; people could see that their military boots had no soles. It only took a little kiełbasa and pork fat for them to let you across. Nevertheless, later on Poles hiding in the grain fields did hear rifle bullets whizzing past nearby. In time, these excursions became impossible.

A lithograph by Napoleon Orda showing a view
of Korets in the mid-nineteenth century.

I remember clearly—and it was 1930, I was seven at the time—my mother at home, grieving deeply. News had come from the prison in Iziaslav that her brother, Piotr Kamiński, had been shot. I kept my ears pricked during conversations at home, though my parents weren't being entirely open. They were afraid I'd run my mouth to my girlfriends. But I knew that my uncle had decided to flee to Poland—because those twenty-five kilometers to the border were very tempting. He was supposed to get help from a certain man by the name of Wysocki, who lived in the border village of Myrutyn. Wysocki hid Piotr in a barn and told him to wait until the time was right. Piotr was keeping an eye on the area through a hole in the wood and noticed Wysocki's wife heading toward the border. After a while, a britzka started rolling up from that direction with a few border guards inside. The woman was with them. Piotr realized Wysocki was a snitch, that the man had encouraged him to flee to collect a bounty. Although the barn was locked, Piotr got outside; he started running away. He didn't make it. Wysocki caught him first. He hit him once or twice. Piotr staggered and blood gushed out. The soldiers caught up to him.

That very day the GPU[2] came to Berezdiv to search Piotr's parents' home and interrogate his close and extended family. Three of his brothers were also

---

2 The State Political Directorate (Gosudarstvennoye Politicheskoye Upravleniye), the Soviet political police from 1922 to 1934, transformed in December 1934 into the OGPU (the Obedinnoye).

arrested: Władysław, Paweł and Jan, as well as all his young male relatives. In one house, a wedding reception was underway; the guests had returned from church and were just sitting down at the table when the GPU entered and hauled away the groom.

Jan later told me that they first put Piotr in an odinochka, a small, damp cell in which he could stand or kneel, but there wasn't enough room to lie down. Then they transferred him to a larger one, which he shared with the local Orthodox priest. Piotr, wanting to protest, decided to stop eating. The guard bringing the food kept saying:

"Eat, Piotr, tebe vsyo rovno, tebe vot, bullet in the head!"

Firing squads were usually organized at night. Once, their cell was unlocked and Piotr and the priest were called out. Piotr went calmly; the priest struggled, and they dragged him by his feet, so he hit his head on the steps. A few shots rang out. Then the key grated in the lock again. Jan thought his turn had come. But the guard just brought Piotr's pants and shirt and said:

"Your brother's been shot, and tomorrow you're being exiled to a camp in the Far East."

Jan spent ten years in the Kolyma camps.

To this day, no one knows what came of Paweł. He was never heard from again.

The fourth of the Kamiński brothers, Władysław, also ended up in a camp—in Vorkuta. After five years, he and a friend, feeling their plight had become unbearable, decided to try to escape. For a while, they kept breaking the crust off their daily bread ration, drying it, and stashing it for the road.

Once they'd built up a small quantity of provisions, they escaped. They covered three hundred kilometers on foot. Their bread ran out; they kept eating mushrooms, but poisoned themselves—then they lay there in the forest, vomiting. Help came out of nowhere. In a pocket they found two more sugar cubes; they each ate one and felt better; they struggled to crawl to a little farmhouse and asked the owner for help. He replied:

"We've got firm orders that if we spot a runaway prisoner from the camp, we absolutely have to alert the authorities—we get money for it. I'm not allowed to help you. If they found out you were here and I didn't stop you, I'd end up right where you're running away from. I wouldn't get out for the rest of my life."

But he gave them a piece of bread and advised them to walk in the direction of the railroad tracks. They finally got there, camouflaged themselves, and waited for a lumber train. Once they'd traveled a ways, they'd jump off before getting to the station, to avoid the watchmen. At night they'd keep struggling along, then once again jump onto a moving train. This is how they finally reached Ukraine.

One night, Uncle Władek knocked on the window of his family home. My mother opened the door, happy but also terrified.

"My sweet boy, I'm sleeping in the kitchen, an NKVD agent is staying in the main room."

Without a sound, she led him into the shed, up to the hayloft, onto some straw. She spent all night on her knees, clutching her rosary, begging God that the NKVD agent wouldn't notice anything.

My uncle needed a passport, which cost a hundred rubles on the black market. Grandma had no money, so they decided together that Władek should walk to Marachivka; maybe his sister, my mother, would be able to help. This conspiracy terrified my parents. They hid Władek in the attic. My father said to my mother:

"For God's sake, Hanka, if someone informs, I'll never get out of prison, you'll work your fingers to the bone with four children, or maybe they'll take you too, and send the children to an orphanage ..."

My father finally walked to Krupets, where my older brother worked for the selsoviet.[3] He was afraid of implicating his son, so he didn't mention the passport, he just asked him to take one hundred rubles from the safe because he needed it urgently, and he'd return it later. Uncle Władek bought the passport, though it didn't do much good—he got caught and was sent back under guard to the same camp he'd escaped.

After a while, when he couldn't hold out mentally or physically anymore, he decided to take his own life, and get revenge on his tormentors in the process.

Many books have been written about the camps; we know how the prisoners were treated, the awful conditions in which they lived, worked, and died there. But now I'd like to tell you how my uncle—Władysław Kamiński from Berezdiv—decided to die.

My uncle worked as a driver in the camp. He drove a truck and sometimes transported tanks full of gasoline. On the camp's grounds there was a solid

---

3 *Selskiy sovet* (Ru.)—the village council.

building made of pine. The ground floor held offices, and upstairs, a cafeteria and official apartments for the administration. Władysław knew that at twelve noon the nachalstvo went to the cafeteria for lunch. In an act of the greatest determination, he decided to open each of the full containers and slam the truck at full speed into the office. He knew the gasoline would spill everywhere and cause an explosion. The building had no other exit, everyone should be killed. He'd worked out all the details, but something always got in the way. For instance, once, as he was getting ready to strike, a column of prisoners appeared unexpectedly in front of the office—he backed down at the last moment.

One day, he was lying on his bunk in the barrack, watching a friend sitting in front of him, bent over and tying on the sole of his shoe with string. Władysław was always very athletic, agile, and knew various circus tricks. Without really thinking, he stretched out his leg and used his toes to pinch his friend in his protruding bottom. The man leapt up, outraged, and gave a smack in the face to his nearest neighbor, who was perfectly innocent. Everyone roared with laughter. The guards came running, and at the sight of their baffled expressions, the prisoners started laughing even harder. It was a long while before they could calm down again.

After that event my uncle lost his desire to commit suicide.

While driving his truck—he was, as it was called, "unconvoyed"—he would often see on the road a young girl walking to work. A couple times he gave her a ride. This was how he met his future wife,

Olya. Olya came from Syktyvkar in Komi country. Fate would later bring them back to Ukraine together, to Klevan near Rivne. And in 1979 on Krakowskie Przedmieście in Warsaw, in front of the Church of the Visitation, they would greet John Paul II.

I go back to my earliest memories. I remember my parents finishing construction on a lovely new house. Marachivka was a beautiful village. Well-tended farms, meticulously thatched roofs, every homestead surrounded by a wooden fence. Green knotweed carpeted the road. The earth was fertile and black as pitch, the meadows were gorgeous, and a river flowed through the village. My father grew potatoes and grain, he sowed millet, flax, and hemp, and planted beets; we had a large vegetable garden. The earth, diligently tended, offered back abundant harvests. Every activity was carried out at the proper time, nothing ever went to waste.

Yet a few of the wealthier farmers had already been exiled—as kulaks—"to the polar bears." None ever returned to Marachivka, and their properties were plundered.

One still living at the other end of the village was Józef Orłowski, a very hardworking farmer; he had beautiful buildings roofed in red tile. One day a group of "activists" arrived from the city. They went to Orłowski's farmstead. My sister and I ran to watch them "dekulakize" him. The activists climbed onto the roofs of the buildings and started dismantling them. Shingles rained down from every direction. The beams were very thick and heavy; they were cutting them up with a saw and throwing the pieces on the ground. They'd brought along an accordion player, who provided cheerful accompaniment; we could hear him all over the village. Józef Orłowski and his wife Walentyna were running around fretfully, carrying whatever they could out of the house. But the demolition was going quickly. Not until the activists were smashing up the ceiling and clay poured down inside did it occur to the Orłowskis that their baby daughter, Fela, had been left in her crib. There were already pillars of dust in the main room, wooden planks and rubble lay around the crib, but by some miracle nothing had happened to the baby.

A few previously "dekulakized" farmers had gotten wolf tickets, documents which forbade them from registering at any address or from getting work. One of our wealthier neighbors, Chotyna, was arrested and never heard from again. His wife and daughter—Tamara and Olga—were sentenced to exile. Their house didn't get dismantled, but a four-year school was set up in it. The Orłowskis were luckier, they stayed in Marachivka. They built a little house on stilts, like a large doghouse, in their garden, and lived in it along with their children, Władek and Fela. They did that for six whole years, until our collective exile to Kazakhstan in 1936.

At the age of seven I started going to school. Once the bitterly cold winter arrived and there was heavy snowfall, I had to stay home. It was impossible to buy shoes, either in Marachivka or the nearby towns. Besides, our entire income from the farm went toward covering our escalating taxes. My father worked hard and after he'd saved up a few rubles, he'd say, "I'll pay this tax too, maybe they won't add any new ones." But right after paying one off, a bill would come for the next, several times higher than the one just paid. In addition to money, we had to hand over grain, cattle, milk, and eggs. From 1930 to 1932, there was no food for the lean season before the harvest. My mother would take out of her chest beautiful woolen pants, dresses, and scarves from her trousseau that dated back to tsarist times (my parents married in 1913) and exchange these gorgeous items for a few gallons of rye or flour. It was always the same until the harvest; difficult, for sure, but we survived somehow.

As soon as it got warm, I ran off to school. My teacher saw I knew how to read and thought I should skip a year. But second grade was the same story all over again: with the first snows I stopped going to school.

In fall, our teacher was replaced with a new one, a girl from the Communist Youth named Horbaczenko. Class was often canceled, because as an activist she went to selsoviet meetings, where they decided who would pay the next tax, whose possessions to auction off, who to take something more from. When my father wasn't able to pay the latest tax, the activists decided to take away our last cow, by then our only support. The cow was very gentle; she gave good, fatty milk and let anyone milk her. We sat in the window and watched them take her away. A few times she turned around and mooed, until finally she disappeared from view.

Every day my mother went to stand in front of the store to buy me shoes. You had to join the line in the evening and wait until morning. She handed over the required five dozen eggs, but the store kept not receiving the goods and so I couldn't go to school.

Once I was staring out the window, waiting for my mother. From a distance I could see that she was coming back empty-handed yet again. When she got home, she said she'd had enough of standing in line, because she didn't believe any shoes would ever arrive. She was sorry she'd given away the eggs for nothing. She sewed up my brother's old shoes for me, unstitched a cushion, and poured the feathers into my stockings, so I wouldn't freeze. I ran happily off to school; my legs were quite warm. The teacher wasn't there, she had a meeting. We hoped she was gone for the day, so we jumped from bench to bench, from the benches to the table, from the table to the floor. After a while our play proved more than my shoes could bear; my stockings ripped and feathers went flying through the air. This made the game even better; we blew feathers and coughed, then suddenly our teacher reappeared. All the children went home, but I had to clean up the classroom. The teacher summoned my older sister Marysia to help me. We fetched water from the well and until late we washed the floors and picked up the feathers with a rag and our hands, though honestly without much success. In the wall newspaper the next day there was a cartoon of us. It showed us disheveled and dirty, with feathers sticking out of our ears and noses. We became the laughingstock of the other children.

That was the end of my education in unfinished third grade.

Then my parents sent me to stay with my grandmother in Berezdiv. I stayed in school there until fourth grade. The teacher often praised me. My new girlfriends were also kind and didn't know anything about the story with the feathers.

Grandma's house stood on the main street, which led to the market square. The square, whose inhabitants were mainly Jewish, formed the center of town. There were oodles of little Jewish stores, and next to them on the open part of the square, farmer's markets were held. When a farmer was marrying his daughter off and was short on money, the Jews would always offer a loan, knowing he'd pay back with interest. Generally relations with them were very good. They were fantastic artisans; so, for instance, to avoid traveling into town, we'd send a wagon from Marachivka to pick up Zejda the tailor with his assistant and sewing machine. The two would stay in a farmer's house, be served kosher food, and over a few weeks make clothes for the entire village. Then they'd get taken back to Berezdiv and both sides would be happy. The tailor would suggest what cut of clothing to choose, and you wouldn't have to go to town for accessories. Zejda also sewed me a coat out of my mother's skirt. I felt bad for her, because Mama looked very stylish in it. It was a long, olive-colored skirt from her single days, the waist pulled in by a wide belt with a decorative buckle, and ending at the bottom with ribbons sewn horizontally around, as if painted with a thick brush.

When Mama was still a young girl, she used to help her Jewish neighbors on Shabbos: lighting candles, fetching water, and lighting the stove, because, as we know, their religion forbade them from doing any kind of work on that day. My grandma would get visits from a Jewish woman she knew, Całycha; oftentimes they'd talk for hours. Wealthier Jews paid Całycha to mourn at funerals and pray at graves; she would place her ear to the ground to listen for what the dead person was saying, and then convey their words to the family. Yet the dead person wasn't always talkative enough and Całycha would come to the same grave several times. I know she once took part in an amazing Jewish ritual: on a particular day, all the Jews in the area would make their way to the river; they knew that on that day an evil spirit would seize one of them, whoever couldn't see their reflection in the water. At one point a tumult and general commotion would go up, the wind would howl and in the general uproar someone would go missing. That time it was Całycha who disappeared. A few weeks later she turned up at grandma's again, changed and haggard.

Marachivka had a little Jewish store too, where my mother would send me for soap, laundry bluing, salt, pepper, or laurel leaves, cinnamon, and sometimes even saffron.

My father had a Jewish acquaintance by the name of Herszko, a distillery owner. Sparrows were the bane of his existence; huge flocks of them would descend on the grain for making vodka. During the revolution, the Bolsheviks smashed up the distillery and pure spirit poured out of the vat into the stream.

The whole village ran to scoop it up. Herszko looked in despair at his ruined distillery, but to my grandfather he said:

"At least the sparrows will leave me alone."

Soon hunger started nagging at us. Grandma kept saying:

"Eat your fill, child, don't worry, I'll go into town and the Jews will give me bread on credit."

The whole winter was like that. People trusted one another, they knew that in summer the debt would be repaid with interest—in the form of onions, garlic, or beans. But in time the Jews, too, started wanting for bread. And then the credit ran out. Grandma couldn't get anything anymore. My parents came from Marachivka and told us there was a horrible famine in the village, people were dying. Meanwhile, day after day, brigades of activists would go around the houses tearing up floors and searching for hidden food.

In Berezdiv, too, everyone was tormented by hunger; fewer and fewer children were coming to school, and the teachers had nothing to eat either. Everyone spoke only of famine, and about eating through all their hidden reserves. Sometimes someone still found some old beans from a few years ago in a shed or in the attic, but before long there was nothing left to be found. Nothing could be bought or borrowed—not in town nor in the countryside. Everywhere it was the same. In the towns, lines stood in front of the stores day and night, and when a little bread turned up, people would squeeze in so hard that someone was often suffocated to death. Grandma finally said to Mama:

"Take the child, maybe in the country you'll get

something faster, because here people are dying of hunger."

No one waited for the end of the school year, no one had the strength any longer to study or to walk to school.

I went back to Marachivka. The village was sad, there were no children playing in the street. Only increasingly predatory brigades, notionally from the Party, but actually from the police, were going around the houses and searching for food.

They kept creating collective farms, known as kolkhozes. Many farmers handed over their horses, wagons, and plows to them—then the horses went hungry, and the plows lay there in the rain, rusting. Then after a while people got together and en masse went to the kolkhoz farmyard to take what was theirs—and so this collective form of agriculture once again became a fiction. Yet after a while the authorities' grip tightened and the more skittish villagers kept going back. The first to pledge themselves were the poorest and the laziest, but before long many good farmers also had to join the kolkhoz. Those who still resisted were tormented with constant home searches, though it had been a long time since there was anything to eat. Mama went around the wealthier villages to trade a beautiful coat or dress for a few potatoes or a cup of lentils, but soon no one would even give her clothes a look.

At school in Marachivka they sometimes made zacierki, a soup made of small, plain dumplings in water, for the children who were still strong enough to come to class. I came too: many people were sitting and waiting for someone to bring a wagon with flour, but no one did and the whole time a gallon of water was boiling pointlessly away. Another day an activist brought us a little flour; one of the mothers kneaded the zacierki and started tossing them into the salted water at a rolling boil; in a few minutes, the water clouded up and larger or smaller dumplings floated here and there. Someone said only those children whose parents had signed up for the kolkhoz had the right to get soup. But the new teacher, very pretty in a navy-blue dress with red pinstripes, poured some for everyone without exception.

My deskmate was Helenka Stelmach. As we were eating the soup I saw she was only sipping the water, and when she came across a larger dumpling, she'd spit it out into a piece of newspaper. I asked why she was doing that, why she wasn't eating. She told me it was for her mother, who hadn't eaten anything in a week, wasn't strong enough to walk, and was lying in bed all swollen from hunger. I felt embarrassed, because I didn't know the last time my mother had eaten. Hela's mother soon died—at that time people were dying in large numbers, all around. On the way to school a young fellow, Omełka, was lying down on some wood planks. The next day I spotted him in the same position; his mouth was leaking some pale-pink fluid that attracted swarms of flies, crowding all over his now-dead eyes, nose, and ears. People were very weak and no one had the strength to dig graves.

Our father was summoned to the selsoviet.

"Waśkowski, sign up for the kolkhoz, you'll get a little flour."

My father was ready to give in, but Mama resisted (people in the village said that anyone who joined the kolkhoz was selling their soul to the devil). She brought in wheat from the garden that hadn't yet formed ears, boiled it in a pot with some willow leaves, and kept saying it would make us strong, maybe we'd get through until the harvest, we'd sown wheat and rye, after all. But it didn't make us strong and we started swelling up. Mama sent me to Aunt Antoszczycha, who lived in the center of the village.

"She's in the kolkhoz, there they get dumpling soup to eat, you'll help with housework, look after the baby; she'll give him food, so you'll get something too."

I went to my aunt's; all day my uncle was plowing earth at the kolkhoz and I rarely saw him. Sometimes he'd give me the foot wrappings he wore with his bast shoes. I'd wash them in the river; they were stiff with blood and sweat, they stank.

Day after day, my grandfather would walk to the forest with two sacks and pick willow leaves. He'd return exhausted, but with the sacks full. Then we'd spread out our bedsheets in the yard and dry the leaves, and next crumble them or mash them in a mortar. One large sack gave us a couple cups of powder. For as long as we had bran, we'd add a handful of it to this willow flour and bake flatbreads. Later there was no bran, and pure willow flatbreads didn't come out so well. This bread gave many people, including my cousin Teofila, awful, persistent constipation.

In spring of 1933, life slowly ground to a halt. Movement in the town and countryside distinctly ceased. People no longer had the strength. Children, hungry and weak, sat at home. They didn't go to school or even outside.

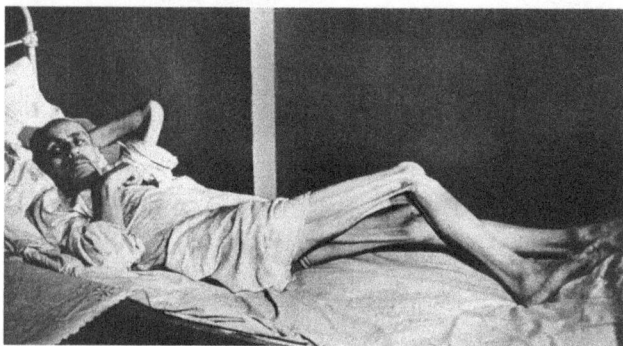

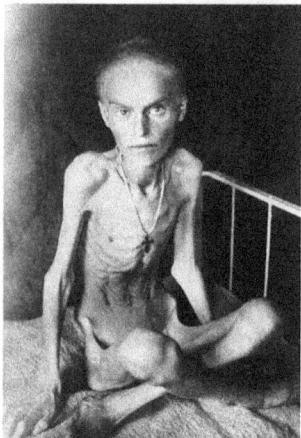

Victims of the Great Famine.
In the land of the most fertile soil in Europe
from 1932 to 1933, three million people died of hunger.
Some sources give a much, much higher figure.

After I returned from Berezdiv, the Orłowskis' dekulakization took place. An auction was held, in which all their movables were sold for next to nothing. The buyers were government officials no one knew. But the villagers bought a few pieces of equipment, to return to their owners afterward.

Soon our house was also auctioned, along with almost everything in it. Yet we could stay there in the meanwhile. My father mowed some straw, dried it, and laid it on the floor of the main room. From then on we slept on straw, and I have pleasant memories of the first night we spent like that. We romped around in the straw a very long time and neither of our parents scolded us. We still had pillows, quilts, and a few things rescued from the brigades busy dekulakizing the village.

It was no mean feat hiding anything from them. They knew how to sniff out even the tiniest sack of grain, the flimsiest bit of clothing hidden in an attic or buried in the ground. These groups were made up of anywhere from a handful to a dozen or more "hepchyks."[4] First they would comb through the house and all the other buildings, without overlooking the smallest nook. Then they would turn to the yard and the gardens. Equipped with metal spears, they would pierce the ground, hoping to hit upon some buried treasure. The spear tips had a kind of little furrow, in which, if the hepchyk had come across something, they'd find a few little seeds of grain, a bit of a feather, or something else. Then they'd dig up that spot and seize the desperate farmers' sack of rye or down quilt.

---

4   A Ukrainian expression for GPU agents.

Our neighbor Paszyńska was disabled and couldn't stand up on her own. She hid two sacks of buckwheat underneath her own body. One hepchyk quickly worked out where he might find some loot. He got the better of Paszyńska very quickly. He came triumphantly out into the yard, joking and laughing: "I'm looking all over the house until suddenly I see St. Nicholas in a painting, nodding to me and pointing at Paszyńska's backside."

One of these brigadiers usually specialized in the "psychological" side of the operation. As the home and garden were searched, he'd keep a watchful eye on the victims' faces. If he noticed a shadow of anxiety or hesitation, he'd immediately signal to his buddies that they were near their target. Then they'd redouble their efforts, which usually met with success.

These searches for plunder deprived people of their last remaining food. The population had already been robbed of their other resources, such as savings in gold. Through various means, the new government very successfully stripped its citizens of everything for its own benefit. Gold coins with the tsar's portrait had in fact already been removed from circulation, but in the towns, stores would pop up where you could use them to buy flour, buckwheat, or even pork fat. The famine was beginning and people who had gold went to these stores and traded it for food. Very often the unfortunate customer hadn't even made it home before the GPU was already there, demanding gold coins from his wife or members of his household. Snitching ran rampant, but the hepchyks would frequently demand gold from someone who had none at all. They'd lock the person up in jail and often use torture, such as squeezing fingers in doors or sticking needles under fingernails, to force confessions. At the same time they'd go to the wife, declare that her husband admitted to owning gold, and order her to hand it over. Only after he'd come back home did it usually turn out this was a ruse, and the suffering and endurance had been all a waste.

My mother's aunt lived not far from Berezdiv, in the village of Krasulia. When her husband was arrested, one of the hepchyks, pretending to be generous, warned her that her husband had confessed to concealing gold; he advised her to get rid of it right away and hide it somewhere else. My great-aunt obeyed. As she was returning from the garden with the unearthed gold, several men burst into the yard. She managed to flee into her house and bolt the door from the inside. But they smashed down first the front door and then the cellar door, where my great-aunt was trying to hide. They brought a sickle and threatened to cut her head off unless she handed over the coins. The desperate woman cried out:

"So cut it off then!"

The furious hepchyk threw himself on her, knocked her to the ground, and started kicking with all his might. My great-aunt was a stout woman, strongly built and powerful. She thought she might be able to defend herself and charged into the fight. She aimed for their groins, thereby incapacitating two of them. The third she attacked with some piece of domestic equipment and split his head open. She would have finished them off if the one with the smashed head hadn't made it out to the yard and passed out there. There were another two men standing in the road by the gate, holding onto her neighbor, who, having heard my great-aunt's screams, rushed over to help her. There was no one else around, since our relatives lived in a settlement far from the village. Now these two threw themselves on my great-aunt. They gave her a serious beating and took the gold. Soon her house was auctioned. My great-aunt and her husband were ordered to move at least one hundred kilometers from the border with Poland.

My father's brother Antoni lived in Marachivka with his wife, Maria, who went by Antoszczycha, their three children, and grandpa Piotr. As I've mentioned, in summer my parents left me with them. I was meant to look after my baby cousin, Kazio, who was a few months old. At this time my uncle and aunt were working on the kolkhoz. When they departed in the morning, they always left a small pot of semolina porridge with milk. My aunt would tell me:

"Make sure the older kids don't eat that, it's only for Kazio."

Yet she was barely out the door before all my thoughts started revolving around that little pot. For a while I'd try to control myself; finally I'd put a stool by the stove and take a few sips. The pot was no longer full, so I'd add some water and … have a little more.

Sometimes my aunt would bring a handful of grain from the kolkhoz, which she'd make into barley soup.

In the towns in the area, sometimes a little bread would get delivered to the stores. Then the evening before, a crowd would start besieging the store. But only the strongest were able to push to the front. In Slavuta, one of these deliveries always left a few corpses in front of the store, people suffocated and trampled in the battle for bread. No one in the village had the strength anymore to try their luck in a "line" like that.

Soon I had to go back to my parents. Always, as I was walking up to the house, my youngest brother would run out to greet me. This time there was no one. The yard was empty and seemingly lifeless. Only after some time did my mother open the door. At first I couldn't recognize her; her face was puffy and shiny, her legs like two logs. My father looked the same. He was lying in the garden, not far from a field of wheat that had sprouted ears but no grains yet.

My other brother, Władek, and I decided to go back to our aunt's. We figured the cupboard that was always locked might hold some food. Across from her house was the homestead of a wealthy farmer named Zadorożny, sealed off tight with a tall palisade fence. We hoped we might get something from him. We walked not down the street, but through the gardens, along the river. There was no trace of anything edible, not vegetables or fruits or leaves. We were approaching the Zadorożnys' yard when in a thicket we found a chicken nest, and inside ... seven eggs! We drank one each. The rest Władek took back home, and he told me to keep an eye out in case the hen returned to her nest.

In that most difficult time, when death was circling our home too, a foal unexpectedly returned to us from who knows where; one that had been confiscated along with our horses. My father, though swollen and barely able to stand, decided to slaughter it. Władek helped him, while my mother stood guard on the road in front of the house. This sort of thing could get you sent to Solovki Prison.

Everything worked out, we lit the stove and threw a large piece of meat into a pot. We hid the rest. At the same time, my mother burned a cotton rag next to the house to mask the smell of the meat. The whole thing happened at night. Each of us kids drank a little bit of the broth; right away, our eyes lit up. In the morning we each had a bowl of proper stock.

The next day one of our neighbors, Kobylański, came over. His dog had dug up a hoof and was munching on it with great relish in the yard.

We shared the foal meat with the Kobylańskis, some other neighbors, and my aunt's family. Władek maintained if we hadn't stumbled across those eggs, we wouldn't have been strong enough to kill the foal.

The meat lasted a few weeks. Meanwhile the grain had started to ripen. My mother cooked soup with it. Every day, we had more and more grain. We had bread again.

This was—as I've mentioned—in 1933. A significant share of the population of Marachivka starved to death. Many, like us, barely escaped with our lives. Meanwhile there were villages where no one survived. That's how it was in those days. Not only in our area—all over Ukraine. The authorities soon announced that they had achieved complete, voluntary, and universal collectivization. There were no more yedinolichniki, independent farmers. Everyone worked on a kolkhoz.

The system of pay on the kolkhozes was based on so-called labor days. One labor day equaled reaping thirty sheaves of grain with a scythe. Our aunt, who was a healthy and strong woman, and had several small children to feed, wanted to earn more. In a single day she reaped sixty sheaves. In view of that, the next morning it was announced on the kolkhoz that one labor day now equaled sixty sheaves. Meanwhile many, weakened and ruined from starvation, couldn't hit that quota even in a week.

I went back to fourth grade in Marachivka. To my great joy our hated teacher Horbaczenko had left, and a woman had arrived in her place who was kind and generous to us. Once when my father got sick, she sent him a doctor from Slavuta.

Although the school in Marachivka had seven grades, they sent me to fifth grade in Slavuta, since they were starting up what people called a Polish school there. The principal was named Sokołowski. He lived on campus with his wife, who would often sit out in the garden. She had a beautiful, pale face and large black eyes partly hidden by long lashes. She wore beautiful dresses. We'd come to the garden to get a look at her and often we saw her spitting out, or rather vomiting up, large clots of blood. She would smile and say to us:

"Sit further away, a little further."

We didn't understand at the time what was going on. We thought she didn't want our company.

Palace of the Sanguszko Princes in Slavuta.

The school and dormitory stood next to the Church of St. Dorothy, across from the Palace of the Sanguszko Princes, which was encircled by a magnificent fence with iron spears, and had been partly destroyed by the Bolsheviks. At that time it contained a hospital probably founded by Prince Roman Damian Sanguszko. He was the subject of many stories in our area. Everyone knew exactly what he looked like: he was an old man of impressive bearing, with a long gray beard. Every day many people would wait for him by the gate in the palace fence as he walked out, always at the same time, to go to the nearby administrative rooms or to St. Dorothy's. He would patiently hear out the whole

Prince Roman Damian Sanguszko (here without a beard),
tortured to death in Slavuta in 1917 at the age of eighty-six.

multitude of petitioners; he always helped when
help was truly needed. He achieved more for the
surrounding populace than any labor unions could
today; as well as factories and workshops, he
founded schools, hospitals, orphanages, and relief
funds; for his retired workers, he set up a "care
home" amid the palace buildings. In Marachivka

the prince owned large grain stores; in 1915 they were gutted by fire, and in retrospect it's hard to say whether this was the result of some military action or rather a harbinger of revolution. My older brother Władysław was born at this time. He had a birthmark on his leg in the shape of a flame; of course, the women we knew thought it was the result of my mother seeing that fire. My grandfather, Piotr Waśkowski, told the story of Prince Roman Damian's death; nowadays I can't render a verdict on whether he witnessed it, or was merely repeating what everyone must have said. On that tragic day, in fall of 1917, he was barbarically dragged from his palace and led through the town to the bridge over the Horyn. He was meant to be thrown from this bridge into the river. Even though by then he was eighty-six years of age, he put up a strong resistance. This was clearly more than the criminals could handle and

The Sanguszko Palace in Slavuta:
riding out into the palace courtyard.

they finally bayonetted him to death. For a long time afterward, people would leave crosses by the bridge.

Once my father visited me; he brought a little food and left me money for a dress. He'd learned in town that there was meant to be some fabric for sale. Sure enough, a huge line had already formed outside the store, and I joined it too. When the doors opened, suddenly a dense, swirling crowd formed, with many strong men pushing their way inside. They shoved out or trampled over anyone in their way. For sale was one roll of flannel. The fat, ruddy saleswoman, whose corpulence had somehow not suffered from the recent famine, kept measuring out fabric and tossing it here and there over our heads. At any moment I could be trampled to death or suffocated. I started fighting desperately to get out of the crowd. When I finally did, it took me a long while to get a grip on myself again. I returned to the dormitory barely alive.

One day not long afterward my geography teacher came to see me; she said that at the train station, amid the crowd of Poles being exiled to Donbas, she'd seen my aunt Rozalia Ihnatkiewicz with her husband and daughter.

"If you want to say goodbye to them," she said, "you have to go straight to the station."

The train station was three kilometers outside the city. By the time I arrived, it had already gotten fairly dark. Sleet was falling. I found my aunt on one of the many wagons. Wrapped in a black shawl, she was sitting there, soaking wet, her face changed. For a long time she hugged me to her, kissed me, and squeezed me. The train cars for deportees weren't meant to leave until morning; amid hugs and tears, my aunt sent me back.

"You'll get wet, freeze, and get sick," she said. "Go back to the dorm. Once the train cars get here we'll be better."

I never saw her, Uncle Franciszek, or their daughter Tulcia again. Later we learned that my uncle worked in a mine, but he was soon taken away by the NKVD. Sometime later my aunt decided return with Tulcia to Ukraine. The police arrested her on the train. Daughter and mother were separated; protests, requests, and lamentations did not help. Tulcia, now in an orphanage, wrote a detailed letter to my grandmother in Berezdiv recounting these events. She thought her mother was in prison. A few months later a telegram arrived in Berezdiv from a psychiatric hospital: "Mental patient Rozalia Ihnatkiewicz is suffering from advanced tuberculosis; her condition is grave." We never received notification of her death. In any event, soon there would be no one who could receive the message. Our whole family was sent on the next transport deep into Russia.

In 1936, when I was in sixth grade—barely about twenty kilometers from the closed and all-too-well-guarded Soviet-Polish border—we often heard talk that the Soviet authorities were systematically exiling Poles far to the east. New transports of people in freight cars kept showing up at the train stations. In June, when classes were still in session, my mother came to see me. She had to take me home because our turn had now come. Twenty-five families were exiled from Marachivka at that time, exclusively ethnic Poles.

At home I found a government official, who had been living with us for a few days and was working on preparing our group. One by one, he summoned all the families assigned to deportation. He said to my father:

"You're to hand in your identity documents; where we're sending you, you won't need them; you'll be trudopereselentsy,[5] that means you're not going to prison, but to work. You must take your son and daughter; you can bring anything with you that you like. You'll get three poods[6] of flour for hardtack; you need to stock yourselves up with food for three or four weeks. You'll ride kolkhoz wagons to the railroad."

So my mother baked bread and made hardtack. We didn't know what day the horse wagons would come for us. I would climb up high in a tree and observe the men who'd been guarding us for some time now. In the evening, the official would arrive on a horse; the guards would give him an account of what was going on in the village: if anyone was running away, objecting, protesting ... One evening, hanging around the guards and asking them questions, I heard snatches of conversation:

"Kogda zavtra budut soprotivlyat'sya, svyazat' i na podvodu."[7]

---

5   In a free translation: labor exiles.

6   About forty-nine kilograms total.

7   Russian: "If tomorrow they object, tie them up and stick them in the wagon."

The following day, right at dawn, the wagons arrived. Over a dozen armed escorts supervised loading and lining up the wagons. We expected we'd head toward Slavuta, because the nearest station was there. But that wasn't the case. Our convoy went in the opposite direction and didn't stop until Maidan-Vyla station. It was thirty kilometers from Marachivka, while Slavuta was only fifteen. We thought this was an additional measure of caution, taken to hinder any possible escape toward the Polish border. We were ordered to disembark not right at Maidan-Vyla itself, but a little further along, in a field, where wood had been chopped and stacked. We camped out amid this firewood for seventy-two hours. The days were scorching while the nights were very chilly. There was no water and everyone relieved themselves wherever they could. Multitudes of flies appeared. Food supplies spoiled at lightning speed and the majority had to be thrown right out.

Meanwhile exiles were brought from other towns as well. By the end of the fourth day, the transport was ready, the train cars were in place and the load-in began. These were freight cars. Each one was designated for eight families. On each side, above and below, were bunks made of wood planks. The families with us included the Orłowskis, the Malinowskis, and the Chmielewskis. The little children mainly got the upper bunks; the beds, of course, leaked, so a few times the children would wet the bed and it would drip on us, forcing us to relocate to the upper bunk.

For the first week, the train moved very quickly,

the stopovers were brief. We didn't always manage even to collect water from somewhere, and most of us had only hardtack left to eat. A few times, during a stopover, we'd light a campfire next to the train and cook barley soup. Often someone got lost and was left behind; yet there were many guards along the route, who would put the stray onto the next transport and at the following stop they'd be re-united with their people.

Once we had the Volga behind us, and then the Urals, the stops grew longer and longer. Sometimes they lasted three days, sometimes even more. During one of them, in Zlatoust, they took us to a bathhouse. We had to take all the clothing we had with us to be disinfected. It was very difficult to push our way into the bathhouse itself. Everyone got only one basin of water. Many people returned to get another. The guardswomen who were meant to monitor the water rationing couldn't tell who was coming back, because we were all as naked as God made us. After this "bath" we were told to line up to collect our clothes. We waited there stark naked. Our clothes were finally returned to us, still warm; anyone who had a fur or sheepskin coat got back a stiff shell that immediately dissolved into dust.

Our journey, begun on June 1, 1936, reached its end on the twenty-first—at the place where the tracks ended. The last station was called Taiynsha.

ON THE STEPPE

We unloaded our belongings from the train and waited for the trucks.

Around us there was nothing. No buildings, no traces of humanity, no trees or bushes. Only dry, yellow, prickly grass. Apart from that, the air was clear and visibility was perfect, except we could see nothing but the horizon. After a while we noticed some largish balls rolling gently around the steppe. These—it later turned out—were a plant known here as a perekoti-pole, with a round shape and very weak roots. The wind often uprooted them and they rolled endlessly into the immeasurable distance.

That very day, there was a solar eclipse. Suddenly it grew dark; fearing the worst, we waited for it to pass. Then true dusk fell. After the heat of the day, a great chill came over us. In the morning it grew hot again. The next military transports arrived. Then later, finally, the trucks came. They started taking us off in different directions. The commandant rode in the first truck, next to the driver. We took a dirt road to the village of Kellerovka, about sixty kilometers from the end of the railroad tracks. From there, we drove on nothing but grass. It was very dry, tall, coarse. When we finally stopped, the commandant got out and cried:

"Vykhodite! Zdes' budete gorod stroit'!"[8]

From the cab he took out a wooden peg with *Gurt Nagilny* written on it. He tried to drive it into the ground, probably as the central point of the future gorod, but the earth was hard as stone, so he just tied the peg to the tall, coarse grass.

---

8   Get out! You're going to build a town here!

That same day, around fifty families were transported there. Like us, they came from Volhynia, from villages neighboring ours. One transport after another was driven off in different directions and deposited on the steppe. The commandant assigned each of these clusters a number: 1, 2, 3, etc. Later, I don't remember why, we named our settlement Chernigovka.

We spent the night on the grass. Some of us sat on furniture we'd brought. We were afraid of wolves, and the night was spent singing hymns. I remember particularly clearly the much-repeated "Serdeczna Matko."

The next day, two Kyrgyz men arrived, transporting twenty large canvas tents. Each one needed to hold twenty to twenty-five families. Inside there was a little space left for an aisle, and the commandant placed one family after another on either side. Each family was assigned a small area, measured per head. There were six of us, so we got 1.5 square meters. If we wanted to cram into that space, we all needed to lie down at the same time, and it was impossible to roll over. As a result many people, like my older brother Władek, spent the nights in the open air. But it was a little warmer in the tent and several people could fit under the same quilt.

Not far from the tents we found the only well in the area. We soon discovered it was badly polluted, filled with a lot of refuse of various kinds. We pulled out animal corpses, rotted cattle skins and hooves. Finally at the bottom we found water. It was brown and stank horribly, but even that odor didn't stop us from drinking. By then the thirst was unbearable. Our water supplies had run out; our mouths felt bone-dry.

The commandant didn't appear until the third day. He informed us it was forbidden to drink water from a Kyrgyz well. We had to wait one more day for a technician who would show us a place where there was water. But when this much-anticipated person arrived, far too late, it turned out that there was no water in the area at all! Some was found three whole kilometers away. Work started immediately. The men quickly removed the first layer of ground, overgrown with grass. Lower down, there were just deposits of hard clay, which we had to break up with an iron bar and carry out in buckets. No one stayed in the tents. Everyone did their best to do something, to help, while those for whom there wasn't enough work stood in a large circle around the laborers, reciting the rosary out loud in the intention of finding water. Near the end of the day we finally reached a spring. People threw themselves on top of one another to slake their thirst. The water was fantastic: clean, slightly sweet, fresh smelling. We kept drawing it with a bucket on a rope and drinking nonstop. No one went back to the tents. After a while the water grew cloudy. Even mixed with clay and sand, it still retained its wonderful flavor, which all of us would surely remember to the end of our lives. By the next day, a van was distributing water among the tents. Soon, eight more wells were dug near the first one. There was no longer any shortage of water. But, apart from the wells, there were none of the furnishings that mark even the most primitive human settlement.

Before long, the commandant arrived with new orders. Three hundred meters away from the tents, we were to dig a ditch to relieve ourselves in.

We also dug another ditch, this time close to the tents; this was to be a cooking pit. It had two levels. On the first, upper one, we were to place the pots, and on the lower one, light the fire. While we were busy with these activities, many of us started to fall ill. This was from drinking the water from the Kyrgyz well. The sick suffered from bloody diarrhea, ran high fevers, and were badly weakened. None of them were strong enough to make it to the toilet-ditch. The tents were surrounded with feces, mucus, and blood. Seared into my memory were the faces of young children whose sunken eyes had dark blue rings around them; their dried-out tongues protruded from their mouths.

The first to lose a child was Niedaszkowska. She ran around mad with despair, asking everyone in turn:

"Where will I bury my child? There's no cemetery here, there's nothing to make a little coffin with ..."

The commandant designated a place for a cemetery not far from the tents. He also got lumber from somewhere to build a coffin. More accurately—coffins, as before long another several children had died. Yet we didn't have long to wait before the adults also started to succumb. First the elderly passed away, and then people in the prime of life too. There were days when in our five-hundred-family settlement as many as a dozen or more people departed into the foreign, Kazakh great beyond. We were weak and wracked with hunger, thirst, and cold. The remains of our food supplies were now a memory, while here one person's monthly ration was eight kilograms of wheat and not a single thing more. The grains were old, hard, and very bitter, since they contained a great deal of wormwood. The only fuel was cow dung, from a herd that wandered the steppe and were tended by locals. These cow pats—known there as kizyaki—dried very quickly in the wind. We gathered them in sacks and burned them under pots placed on two stones, which were also not easy to find. The wheat we were given, boiled for hours, still remained hard and was clearly indigestible—as we could see all too well everywhere between the tents.

Meanwhile we had much more difficult work in store for us than digging wells. Summer was passing, it was almost high time to prepare shelter for the winter. Exhausted and apathetic, not everyone realized this necessity. The commandant did his best to make us aware.

"This isn't Ukraine," he kept saying. "The frosts come as early as October, so hard that each and every one of you here will be killed. No one will even know there were people here at all. You need to build mud huts."

He didn't mean shelters dug in the ground, but small, solid houses made of steppe clay.

First, after removing the first layer of earth and grass, we had to make a so-called kotlovan. In the middle of a large circle with ten-meter radius we left a thick column of clay, to which we would fix a rotating mixer—a broad, transverse beam bristling with narrow little wheels. The clay in the kotlovan had to be dug fairly deep, and was so hard and compact that we had to break it up with crowbars. Then, using a channel made of a few wooden planks, we poured in water, which women drew from the well with buckets. The older children helped them. The youngest, myself included, cut straw. When the clay in the kotlovan had softened, horses were harnessed and would pull a mixer behind them in a circle. Next, the cut straw would be thrown into the now-mixed clay and the mixing would continue. Finally we'd shovel out this heavy mass, load it onto wheelbarrows, and bring it a short distance to where wooden molds awaited. The rest was up to the women—because everything done so far was the men's duty.

Each mold had room for four samany, mudbricks. The molds had little dividing walls inside that allowed the production of smaller modules. These modules would be a significant element of future construction, getting arranged to form walls, doorways, and so on. Women stood on either side of each mold: first they would wet the inside with rags, and only then put in the clay, pounding it for a long time with their fists. Finally they'd flip the mold over and if the clay was well mixed, moistened, and beaten, the mudbricks would fall out on their own. Though often they didn't want to.

Shaking a mold took enormous effort—one mudbrick, after drying, weighed around sixteen kilograms. And how much could it have weighed wet, still in the mold? It was hellish work, but the mud huts were our only chance of surviving the winter.

A little wood was brought for windows and doors, and reeds for the roofs. Every house was divided in half, making two separate rooms of around three by four meters square. In the corner by the door, a Russian stove was built: your pot of food had to go inside. There weren't enough dry samany, so the walls were damp and soft; sometimes you could stick your finger all the way in.

People kept dying. There was no doctor or medic anywhere. There were no medicines or any sort of medical substances. Pani Kamińska from Berezdiv died during childbirth after suffering for several days. The women who dressed her for the coffin saw a little hand sticking out. Apparently the fetus was in transverse position. We had no midwife (and there was no chance of help from outside) who could have aided Kamińska to give birth and survive.

Later the women no longer gave birth; they had all stopped menstruating.

From time to time stronger and younger people would attempt to escape. There were no guards in Chernigovka and no patrols on the steppe. Little groups of escapees would always head toward the railroad tracks. They would cover the eighty-kilometer distance on foot, bypassing Kellerovka and other settlements on the way. Weary and famished, they would only be caught once they were near the tracks. Anywhere with any transportation links was closely guarded. When more of these desperate people were caught, they were taken back in trucks to the places from which they'd fled.

At this time we were still counting on aid from

Poland. "After all," we said, "they know over there how many Poles have been deported from Ukraine. They have to do something for us, don't they? To try to help …" I even remember part of a poem someone composed, in which a knight rode onto the Kazakh steppes on a white horse with a red cross, to free us from our misery.

Meanwhile we were trying to survive. We would buy grain from the Kyrgyz, grind it into flour, and cook round dumplings with no filling, known as kluski. That was the only food for the whole of the first winter. The temperature dropped to sixty below zero. When a snowstorm kicked up, it would often last three, six, or even nine days. When you poured out a bucket of water, only hunks of ice would hit the ground.

My father, like many others, got night blindness. As he was making his way back to the house in the evening, he couldn't find the door. In the place where a candle-stub was burning, he could only see a dot the size of a seed.

Large numbers of us fell ill with tsynga, meaning scurvy. Nearly all the children my age lost their teeth; mine actually held on, but they would have fallen out if I'd pushed on them with my tongue. I spent almost all winter on top of the stove; I didn't have the heavy felt boots known as pimy. No other shoes could protect against the unimaginable cold we had. Once my brother gave me his pimy so I could walk around a little. It turned out I could barely stand. All my joints hurt; all over my body I had huge, bloody bruises that had appeared spontaneously, without any injury.

Mama and several people we knew decided to go to the village of Rublyovka, about forty kilometers away, and try to buy some food. We had no money; our wage for working on the mudbricks was a wage in name only. For a whole month of backbreaking work my father was paid one ruble and fifty kopecks, at a time when a loaf of bread cost one ruble. For chopping straw, I got three rubles. That was my first paid job in my life. Yet at the end of the day we didn't need money, because the only way to get food was by trading items from our wardrobe.

My mother nearly paid for this excursion to Rublyovka with her life. On the way back they were caught in a snowstorm. They got lost. Their horse was struggling to pull the sleigh and they had to push it. My mother, exhausted, stayed at the rear. Finally she collapsed in the snow and was too weak to get up anymore. Our neighbors went back and with great effort dragged her to the sleigh. Late that night they brought her home, unconscious, cold, and stiff, but fortunately still alive. We rubbed her all over her body and kept warming her up right until morning. She slowly recovered. She hadn't brought onions or garlic from Rublyovka, but she got a few dried potatoes, more resistant to the cold, and some sauerkraut. That sauerkraut is probably the only thing that saved my teeth.

Some who set off for other villages in search of food didn't come back. Only in spring, once the snow began to thaw, did we find their bodies. During a snowstorm you could get disoriented and get lost even on the way to the well. So we'd go to fetch water holding a bucket in one hand and a rope in the other. We'd wrap the rope around a forearm and slowly unroll it as we walked. That allowed us to find our way back home.

We were steadily learning how to live on the steppe. Its permanent inhabitants would explain to us:

"No one will take you away from here, and you can't escape. You need to adapt."

The next summer, further work began. We needed to add a few extra rooms to the house, buy a Siberian cow, gather fuel for next winter. Soon the foyer, separating the living room from the fuel store, was ready, and then afterwards a room for the cow. This sort of structure allowed us to milk our "roommate" in winter without going outside. Collecting cowpats on the steppe was a job for us, the children. They weren't just used for burning in the stove; when mixed with water, they were useful for coating the dirt floors in the houses. Once this blend had dried, it wouldn't crack when you swept it nor give off a bad smell.

All over the settlement, more and more such structures were going up. Apart from the various types of rooms that individual families built, one after another our village gained: a so-called office, a club, a medical center, and also a large, long cowshed—because there was now a kolkhoz—and a school. We knew this would be a school only for the youngest children, grades one through four. Any of the displaced settlers who had graduated seventh grade could become a teacher. Fall was coming and at home we decided I'd take up studying.

One day an opportunity presented itself. A wagon harnessed with a pair of oxen was going to Taiynsha Station for lumber. On the way, there was a village with a school with grades for older children. My mother and I rode there along with another girl my age, Rozalka Rybicka. Once there, it turned out that the principal was away and wouldn't be back for a few days. My mother left us in a house where, in exchange for accommodation and food, we were supposed to help look after the little children. Our hostess was a kind woman who fed us until we were full. The principal came back and we discovered that, as children of displaced persons, we weren't allowed to attend the school. We returned to the house in tears. Our hostess wanted to help us and to intercede on our behalf with the principal. She came back agitated and close to crying. Her husband was afraid of trouble and told us to go straight back to our parents. Before we could even get on the road, some chinovnik[9] turned up in the yard, threatening to fine them for putting us up.

We walked all day without coming across a car, wagon, or any living soul. We were terrified of wolves. We often heard they attacked people, leaving nothing behind but feet inside rubber boots. That evening we reached the village of Lipovka. We asked for lodgings at a whole string of houses. But everyone refused us, explaining they weren't allowed to take in displaced persons. So we sat down by the last house to wait for dawn. We had stopped asking for shelter, but clearly the mistress of the house here

9   Government official.

was more compassionate than the other villagers of Lipovka; she invited us inside and served us potatoes with sweet, hot milk. She spread out a quilted jacket on the floor, on which we slept like logs until morning. In the night I felt her covering us with something.

We didn't have a watch, nor did our hostess, but the sun was already high as we left Lipovka. In early evening we reached Chernigovka. After that journey our hip joints and feet hurt for a long while.

Our next attempt to resume our education ended in success. In September 1937, Krysia Zgrzybłowska, Walentyna Otawczyc, and I found ourselves in the village of Letovochnoye, twenty kilometers from Chernigovka. There was a seven-grade school there. We rented a place to live from the Marchlewskis, a couple who were also displaced. We each paid them ten rubles a month. Like everyone, they only had one room. Pan Marchlewski knocked together a cot out of a few planks of wood, on which we girls all slept together.

But before that occurred, I sat out the 1936–37 school year on top of the stove in Chernigovka, making thread into lace that could be used to edge a handkerchief, to trade later for food. I was afraid I'd find school difficult, and although I could have enrolled in seventh grade, I signed up for sixth. This put me two years behind. The school principal was a Russian named Sevastochnov; he taught math and geometry and spoke in Russian. Biology and geography were taught by a couple, the Olchowskis; they spoke Polish, but they did their best to hold classes in Russian. The result was a blend of Russian, Polish, and Ukrainian, with the latter predominating. In this respect, it was like Volhynia—we really only spoke Polish once in a blue moon. We did pray in Polish, but we conversed in Ukrainian. Meanwhile at school in Letovochnoye we would do Russian dictations, but no one knew the language well.

Once a week we'd go home to get food. Usually we'd bring a little bread and hardtack, sometimes pierogies with sugar beet preserves, and in winter also a supply of frozen milk. We'd freeze it at home in shallow pots, which we only had to put outside the house door for a few minutes before bringing them back in. From the pot, out would fall a frozen disk. We'd take a whole sack of these disks to Letovochnoye. In the morning, before leaving for school, we would put one of them in a pot and before long we were drinking warm, fresh milk. The local cows didn't give much of it, but it was very rich.

Once, when we girls were on our way back from Chernigovka and already getting close to our village, we decided to take a little rest. We felt incredibly sleepy and thought a short nap in the snow would do us good. There was no wind, the snow was fluffy and soft. Suddenly we felt blistering blows. A man on a horse was lashing us with a whip and shouting:

"Get up! Get up!"

Not understanding what was happening, we obediently walked a little further, but we were so very sleepy that we lay down on the snow again. The man, who'd ridden off a short ways, nevertheless turned around and started whipping us again. We finally regained consciousness and dragged ourselves all the way home. I couldn't work out what had happened to us. Only late in the evening did the man appear in our village. He somehow found our house and explained to my parents (he didn't have to say much!) that we must have been freezing in the snow; that he couldn't wake us up and the only way he was able to persuade us foolish girls to keep moving was with his bullwhip.

"The silly things would have frozen to death—a stone's throw from their own village."

The school year passed and I returned home for summer vacation. The faces of my parents and siblings were badly ravaged by the freezing steppe wind. All winter long they had to go do so-called snow retention. We already knew that when spring came, we'd have to plow the steppe. To keep even a little moisture in the soil, the displaced settlers had to sweep the snow into heaps, often leaving small drifts behind. But as often as not, arriving at the same spot the next day, they'd find no trace of the previous day's work. The steppe gales swept the snow clean, with only dry grass poking out. Even so, almost every day they had to go do this "zader-zhaniye snega."

In spring, the tractors came and plowed the never-before-cultivated earth. They planted a wheat variety known as kubanka. Of course we couldn't sow winter wheat. That summer was incredibly wet. The locals said summer often passed without a single rain and became so dry it was scary. Then the sun would burn the grain completely even before an ear could appear.

Graduation certificate from sixth grade in Letovochnoye, Kellerovka Raion, North Kazakhstan, 1938.

The heavy rain meant the harvest this time was fantastic; the wheat grew two meters tall; the ears were also long and the grain, large and lush. Threshing machines arrived; afterward, enormous piles of grain lay in the fields. A few dump trucks' worth of grain was also piled in front of each mudbrick house. Everyone said that such a harvest happened once in many years. We had to make reserves. But there were no storehouses. In our homes we made airtight compartments where we kept the grain. The one in our house took up a quarter of the main room and, for want of space, we slept on it. But large amounts of grain were going to waste in the fields. Our settlement's storage possibilities were completely used up and it depressed us to see this seemingly happy circumstance transition into the absurd.

At this time a feldsher, a type of medic without a full doctor's qualification, was sent to Chernigovka: Nina Bobel. We'd had a clinic for a while, but without a staff it was one only in name. The feldsher brought with her a little dressing material. Her work mainly consisted of dressing frostbite and wounds. In the neighboring village of Krasnaya Polyana there was something like a sick ward. There were sometimes typhus patients, including my mother—they got taken there. Given the lack of medicine and tools, the feldsher herself didn't have too much work in our village. The head of the kolkhoz, Kornatowski, started to accuse her of completing her duties late, and he claimed patients were spending too much time in the clinic.

Nina Bobel was not a meek person. She said she started work at the right time, since she had a watch and knew what time it was. No one else in the entire area had a watch. Even if someone had brought one to Kazakhstan, long ago they'd traded it for food in more distant, more affluent villages. Nor was there a radio anywhere, let alone a telephone or telegraph. The dispute between the head of the kolkhoz and the feldsher drew in many people from the settlement. Neither side would budge. Someone finally suggested riding a wagon to Kellerovka, where there was apparently a radio receiver. So they did. The next day Nina Bobel and Kornatowski got into a wagon and rode the thirty kilometers to Kellerovka. The trip there and back took all day. To make matters worse it turned out to be fruitless: the radio was broken, and a watch unobtainable even there.

So despite significant efforts the dispute over the time went unresolved.

The school year began. Once again I moved in with the Marchlewskis in Letovochnoye. I was now in seventh grade.

My older sister Marysia had learned to drive a tractor and got a job doing so. Her team had to plow the steppe far from any human habitation. They all would spend the night in lean-tos, sleeping on the ground. They had to plow until the first frost. The effects of this work soon manifested themselves painfully. Marysia came down with myocarditis and arthritis. She spent all winter lying in the root cellar; she had swollen hands and feet, and a very painful contracture in her knee. Meanwhile the myocarditis left behind a serious defect. Years later it would be the cause of her early death.

My younger brother Lucjan went to school in Chernigovka.

My older one, Władysław, worked in the selsoviet there.

One day in winter of 1938, a gathering was meant to take place in the club. Yet a snowstorm blew in and the villagers stayed in their houses. There were only three people at the club: the president of the selsoviet, Błoński; the manager of the club, Lipski; and my brother Władysław. They decided to make the most of the situation; they drank a little vodka and ate some canned food. They reminisced about the old days. Władek, who had always had a lively temperament, at a certain moment grabbed an inkwell and flung it as hard as he could at an enormous portrait of Stalin standing by the wall. It struck the face, making a hole; ink spattered all over the rest. The three friends recklessly determined that since there was a snowstorm and no one was coming, until the morning there was no need to eliminate all traces of this imprudent act. They intended to do so at the crack of dawn, before anyone could work out what had happened. But it was not to be. First the school principal arrived at the club—Gromiński, a German by descent. He quickly summoned the commandant. They formed a commission and wrote a report. They hammered wood planks together to make an enormous crate, big enough to fit the whole portrait (including the frame, it was almost two meters tall). They also threw in, as corpus delicti, the penknife used to open the canned food, and the empty can. They loaded all this into a wagon. Another few activists climbed in and the whole commission set off for Kellerovka. That same day, Władek, Błoński, and Lipski were arrested.

The trial took place on a frigid winter day. My mother took what she could—a large loaf of bread and a piece of pork fat—and went to Kellerovka on foot. On the way, a wagon rolled past her. Riding in it were activists also on their way to Władek's trial. They were wearing sheepskin coats, pimy, and warm leather caps. They knew my mother well; they could see she was struggling along in a miserable coat, with a bundle on her back. They urged their horse on harder, and quickly blew past her.

Władek was sentenced to eight years' hard labor (the prosecutor had requested twelve), Lipski to six, and Błoński to four.

My mother wasn't allowed to say goodbye to her condemned son. But the guard took the frozen-solid bread and pork fat. Immediately after the trial the prisoners were led to the train tracks.

After many difficult stopovers they found themselves beyond the Kolyma River, in the Nagayev Bay region, adjacent to Magadan. Władek worked clearing taiga. It was forced, backbreaking labor. The prisoners would bind tree trunks together to make rafts, and float them down the Kolyma River. The binding would often give way, and the unfortunates would be left on a single trunk, fighting for their lives against the elements.

Later my brother ended up in a gold mine. He survived all those awful years and served out his sentence, plus extra, which was practically a miracle. And ten years later he returned to Chernigovka.

After Władek's arrest and deportation, my parents were broken. When I came from Letovochnoye to Chernigovka on free days, there was no one waiting for me. No one greeted me or asked how I was doing. Their thoughts were with Władek. Alive, or maybe now dead? Or perishing somewhere alone in the bitter cold or underground.

I graduated from seventh grade and went back to Chernigovka. By then we were no longer going hungry. We had good wheat bread, and our cow was giving a little milk. We were trying out planting potatoes. In August, as we were counting the days until we could harvest them, a frost arrived unexpectedly one night. In the morning, nothing was left of the potatoes but black, shriveled little shrubs. The wheat, on the other hand, was abundant. Trucks would take it off to a grain elevator in Sukhotino. Sometimes we'd buy a sheep from the Kyrgyz, though very rarely. Then we'd have a little meat to eat. In 1938, meaning more than two years into our exile, we got our first letter from Marachivka, from Maria Waśkowska, my father's sister-in-law, the same woman whose son Kazio I'd looked after during the famine in Ukraine. She wrote that for the first time she was able to send us a package with onions and garlic. She sent as much as the mail regulations permitted, meaning thirty-two kilos of food. The package was in a wooden crate additionally sewn up with white canvas. What reached us was around ten kilos of onions and a few heads of garlic. My aunt sent thirty-two-kilo packages like that another few times. They contained onions, garlic, and dried apples—a great delicacy, since no fruit trees grew in northern Kazakhstan. That first contact with our hometown was a joyful experience. Unfortunately, it also brought tragic news.

Certificate of school graduation in Letovochnoye, 1939.

We learned that my aunt's husband, Antoni Waś-kowski, my father's brother, had been arrested and put in prison in Slavuta. My aunt had walked there practically every day and asked to see her husband. They didn't let her, not even once. Nor did they even once take her package of food. After some time she learned that her husband, a healthy man in the prime of life, had died in prison. Although Mara-chivka was barely fifteen kilometers from Slavuta, she was never officially informed of his death. Nor was his body returned. An equally tragic fate met my father's other brother, Stanisław. He lived in the nearby village of Nohachivka. He was sent to the same prison, in Slavuta. His family learned that he'd been exiled to the Far East. That was the last news they received, and unofficially at that. They never heard from him again, whether directly or through anyone else.

The news from Volhynia therefore mainly brought deep mourning and, beyond that, anxiety for the fate of the third brother, our father. The Soviet re-gime's terror was not content to exile us to Asia, into the boundless, hostile steppes of Kazakhstan. It started tyrannizing us here as well. NKVD agents would come at night and take men away. Of the peo-ple we knew, they took two of the Rybickis—"Fin-gerless" and "Scrubber"—as well as Iwanicki and Zgrzybłowski.

The arrests were brutal. Most often they took place late at night. Every house had to keep some food and a change of underwear at the ready, though often, in the violent scuffle, they wouldn't manage to take even that. Every day my mother cooked something to eat, but it was harder with the underwear and the clothes. Things sent from Marachivka got torn up. My father no longer had any pants. The only fabric left at home was thick, striped kilim. My mother sewed some pants out of it. When in the evening my father came back from work in them, we discovered the skin on his legs had been chafed bloody.

The days went by. We learned that in Petropavlovsk in northern Kazakhstan there was a three-year feldsher school. I decided to try my luck. I passed the entrance exam without difficulty. The problem came when they found out I was a displaced laborer, a trudopereselenets. Yet the director told me that people born after 1920 who were accepted into a school could try to have this label of displacement removed.

With my heart on my sleeve I headed to the NKVD office. There they told me that if I showed proof of my acceptance to the school I'd be released from the category of trudopereseleniye. But the director replied that he would take me without difficulty as soon as I had the required nod from that terrifying institution. I couldn't contain my fear, yet even so I marched back and forth between the school and the NKVD more than a dozen times, on wobbly legs.

Finally one day I got the emancipation I'd been dreaming of. My joy was boundless. I was accepted to the feldsher school and got a place in the dormitory.

I think that was the first time I felt my life might go more favorably, that I might not remain forever in this cruel, inhuman world to which the Sovietsky Soyuz had ruthlessly condemned us, although we were in no way guilty.

I wholeheartedly thanked God for this unexpected change.

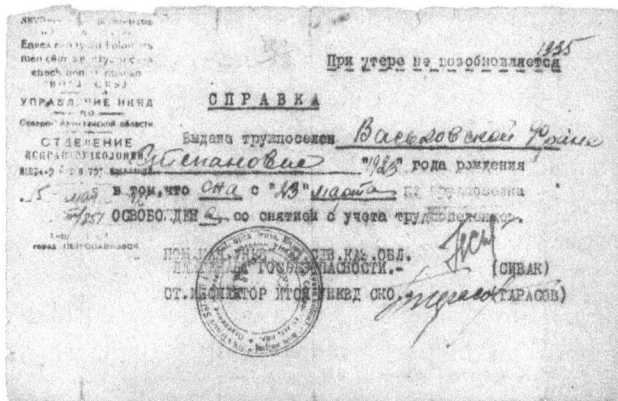

A spravka—the document releasing the author from labor exile status, issued by the NKVD in Petropavlovsk.

I WANT TO BE A DOCTOR

The dormitory stood at 37 Papanin Street. It was a small, wooden building. The bedrooms were on the second floor, downstairs was the kitchen with a large built-in cauldron in the middle. We scooped boiling water out of it to soften our hardtack. There was no cafeteria.

The janitor kept everything tidy. She scrubbed the unpainted wood floor until it was white. She also taught us how to pretty up our bedrooms. To do so, we had to get a hold of a few bandages, unroll them, and add lace, crocheted out of white thread. We'd cover our beds with one of these "bedspreads." To make it more beautiful, on the bottom edge, we attached little balls of cotton wool covered in gauze, hanging on little three-centimeter strings.

To the Soviet authorities at that time, only heavy industry mattered. Acquiring any kind of fabric or clothing bordered on a miracle. The only textiles left in the stores were ribbons. If a person could afford them, they could sew them together and make quite a beautiful skirt. Soon even the ribbons were gone, and only narrow strips of tape remained. Some girls tried to sew skirts out of them. It took painstaking work, patience, and stubbornness, and even then it didn't come out so well, since these garments usually fell apart after a few days.

I really enjoyed the lectures at school. The professors were polite and spoke in a clear, accessible fashion. We had textbooks; there were things to learn from. Starting the very first year, we attended practical lessons in the hospital. This was a true object lesson—and important—for my further education, and maybe, who could say—for my whole life?

Many young people were dying of tuberculosis. They would spit blood, their faces were wax-yellow. They were constantly asking the doctor if they'd survive the next hemorrhage. When we arrived for the following class, we'd find many of them were gone. One I particularly remembered was a young, beautiful girl with long lashes and curly hair. As soon as I got to the sick ward I'd search for her gaze, wanting to make sure she was still alive. Unfortunately that didn't last long.

We examined many X-rays showing cavities the size of a goose egg or even a fist. Doctor Mordwina explained to us that in a few days the tubercle bacilli would attack the artery traversing the cavity; then the vessel would burst, the patient would have a major hemorrhage, and there would no longer be any saving them.

On the pediatric ward, tuberculosis was taking an equally terrifying toll. Many children were suffering from TB meningitis. Those who didn't die returned home with a terrible disability, which was the result of brainstem damage. They lay in beds, most often completely blind, deaf, with all their muscles paralyzed; they could only take liquid food.

Still today, my thoughts turn back to one of the patients from the surgical ward. He was a victim of sarcoma, a very nasty tumor. His arm had already been amputated several times, piece by piece. First to the mid forearm, yet the cancerous tissue kept growing. The second amputation was to the middle of his upper arm. The tumor didn't stop that time either and in a few weeks they had to remove his shoulder joint. In its place was an enormous lump that swelled above his head—to the size of a bucket, stinking horribly, with an enormous amount of purulent discharge.

There were also many patients with advanced stages of brucellosis, with misshapen spines and deformed joints.

In the maternity ward I met a woman who was giving birth for the twenty-fifth time. All her children had survived, and she herself looked absolutely fine.

I was supposed to graduate from feldsher school in June 1942. Yet in June 1941, the "Great Fatherland War"—the war between Germany and the Soviet Union—unexpectedly broke out. The school administration received orders to cut the program short and wrap up the lectures. Feldshers were needed at the front. By December 1941 we had received our diplomas and were sent to various services.

I got orders to depart for Pavlodar in eastern Kazakhstan. When I arrived, it turned out there were many doctors and feldshers there, evacuated from Kyiv, Odesa, and other cities. There was no work for me. So I was sent to the village of Sherbakty. There was a hospital there that was meant to receive wounded soldiers from the front. Three friends and I were put up in the hospital to wait for the expected transports.

It was mid-January, intensely cold; the temperature went down to –60 degrees. There wasn't enough food for the patients who were already there. Nor were there any dressing materials. We slept in an unheated room. The only thing we could buy in the cafeteria was … ice cream sold by weight.

We constantly had stretchers at the ready. We were awaiting future patients—wounded soldiers from the front. We were counting on some food to turn up: flour or bread. Our wildest dreams were some warm kluski or a few tablespoons of kasha. We were constantly thinking about food, which incessantly dominated our imaginations.

But no train arrived. There was no radio, nor did any newspapers reach there. We didn't know what was happening at the front.

I missed Chernigovka. There they got the newssheet *Stalinskaya Pravda*, though with a two-week delay. It was a peculiar pleasure deciphering its propagandistic content and speculating about what was really going on, since we didn't believe a single word. If the paper described the Germans' ruthlessness and cruelty, we saw that as pure propaganda.

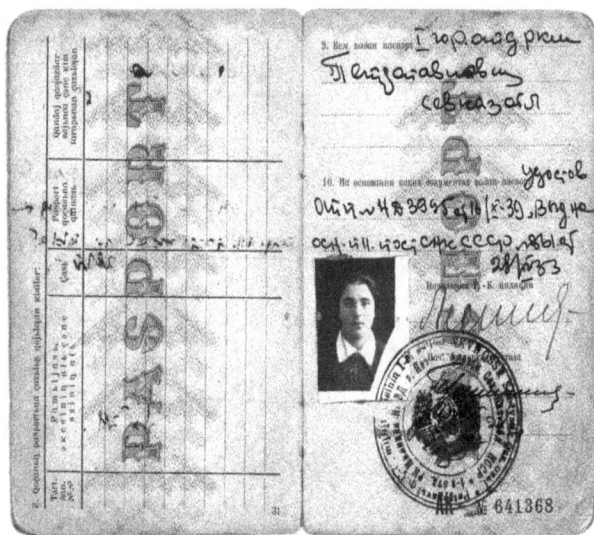

The author's Kazakh passport. The following pages show the names of the towns through which she journeyed: Sadykashy, Kharkiv, Chernivtsi.

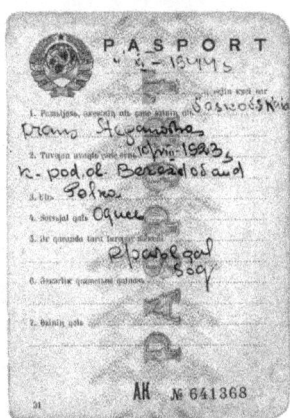

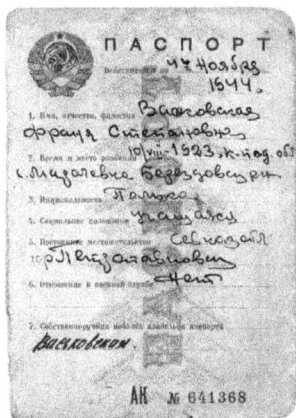

Finally at the end of June 1942, my mother went to Kellerovka. There she learned that the Red Army was in constant retreat. She raced the nearly thirty kilometers back as if on wings. She felt no fatigue, and ran from house to house to share this joyful news with everyone. The more cautious people tried to calm her; they said: "Quiet, don't run around like that, all your running and stupid chatter could get you locked up, and us too." At the same time everyone was happy to hear the news. They thought that once the Germans reached Kazakhstan, we would finally be liberated. We were ready to trust the most savage cannibals, as long as they would free us from the terror, poverty, and hopelessness in which we were living.

My mother had no way of foreseeing that the war would go on as long as it did and take away her youngest, most beloved son.

Back in Sherbakty, we knew nothing. We kept saying: "We're hungry, we're cold, we're far from home."

The local administration informed me that I had been transferred to the village of Sadykashy, ninety kilometers away. I was supposed to wait for them to send a sleigh, a sheepskin coat, and pimy—in other words, felt boots. Without such equipment no one could set out on the road.

When the day came for me to leave, I put on the overcoat they'd allocated me, heavy and stiff, as well as the equally heavy, hard, uncomfortable pimy. Dressed like this there was no way I could clamber up into the sleigh. The driver helped me. Once I was seated he wrapped up my face in an enormous hood and advised me to leave only a little slit to breathe.

"You should be home with Mama," he muttered. "You're lucky there's not a big freeze and it's calm. When the wind kicks up, it's easy to get lost, the horses get weak and you don't meet anyone on the road."

He told me about these nasty adventures when we stopped to rest. Every day we covered thirty kilometers. We slept in villages about that same distance apart.

The local population welcomed us warmly. First our hosts would tell me to keep my overcoat on for a while. I'd only take it off later. They'd give us something to eat and drink, then prepare bedding. They'd feed the horses. One evening they offered me homemade beer, strongly seasoned with salt. It made me throw up violently. As we were leaving in the morning, our host would come outside, look up at the sky, and declare no snowstorms were coming. Then he'd feed the horses and we'd set off. After three such days, I arrived at my destination.

Sadykashy was a village surrounded by a mighty pine forest. The houses stood at the woods' edge, around a large glade, with a long wooden building in the center. It held an orphanage evacuated from Voronezh. Some of its charges had ended up there after losing their parents in the war; other children didn't remember their parents at all. Neighboring buildings served as a kitchen and dining hall, and a third, built of sod, as a laundry. Nearby, separately, was a sick ward. It consisted of two rooms: one designated for sick children, another for a reception office, while I lived in a third. My room had two windows and a beautiful pine floor; inside were a bed and a table.

Evacuated to Sadykashy along with the children were Party officials from Aleksandrovka, near Voronezh. There was a woman there—the first secretary of the raikom[10]—and accompanying her were over a dozen people from her immediate and extended

_____

10 Regional Committee of the Communist Party of the Soviet Union.

family, all women. Their husbands were officers, and one was even a lieutenant colonel. Topovina, the lieutenant colonel's wife, like all the other officers' wives, considered herself a person of privilege. Hence when it turned out scabies was raging among the children, I couldn't count on their help or even their presence. Quickly—so as not to waste time—I separated the healthy children from the sick ones, bringing the ones with fevers to the sick ward. For three days, mornings and evenings, I rubbed tar cream on my juvenile cohort, then lit the stove in the laundry room and washed the children with gray soap. I spent whole days laundering and boiling their underwear, piles of which kept growing at a worrying pace. The older girls would help me put cream on the younger ones, the boys would bring water from the well. Before long the scabies began to subside; here and there we still had cases, but now they were easy to cure. Around this time, after seeing that somehow I hadn't caught it, the secretaries' and officers' wives also started finally helping me. The constant laundering severely damaged the clothing. After a while it was badly shredded and the children had nothing to wear. The orphanage had a reserve of linen and cretonne, rolls of which lay in storage; yet it took the director a long time to make up her mind whether to allocate it for clothing. Luckily we at least had something to eat, mainly kluski with a little clarified butter.

Because when it came to food, the future was uncertain. In 1942 the orphanage received no food rations and we increasingly feared that we'd have to trade fabric for food for the children and staff.

Finally there was no other solution and we started hand-sewing shirts. By chance I also got a hold of a little white linen for a dress. A teacher, Zakharova, embroidered me a modest design on it.

That same winter a group of several dozen soldiers arrived in Sadykashy, including many officers. They lived in Kyrgyz huts and had no shortage of food. Supposedly they were meant to be clearing the forest, but we didn't see them actually working there or even pretending to. One of them courted me. His name was Mikhail Vereshchatsky. He said he came from Moscow, his sister was a doctor and lived in Leningrad.

They soon departed. Word in the village was that they were deserters from the front, and clearing the forest was just a ruse.

A few Kyrgyz villages were assigned to my feldsher clinic. At this time the Soviet authorities had forbidden the locals' nomadic lifestyle. They were meant to settle somewhere permanently and work on the kolkhozes.

The wealthier ones had a lot of blankets, linen, kilims, carpets; some were for covering yourself, others for laying out on the floor. In the daytime they all lay folded up by the walls. For the night they were spread out on the floor on top of one another. They didn't use beds, and chairs also were unknown. But every home had a table, large, round, and on very short little legs. It usually stood in the foyer against a wall, and at mealtimes it would be rolled into the main room. Then the family would sit cross-legged around it on the floor. The staple foods were beef and mutton, eaten almost raw, but very briefly roasted over a fire. The Kyrgyz drank the slaughtered animal's blood while it was still warm. It seems they only acquired the custom of cooking meat from exiles.

Sometimes I'd be invited into a Kyrgyz home. Often, boiling away in a huge pot would be a whole sheep, which would next be placed on an enormous copper tray. The host would share out the meat by hand; he'd place the largest portion, on the bone, before me, as a guest; the family members would get somewhat smaller shares, now with the meat separated from the bone. This dish was called beshbarmak, which means "putting meat in your mouth with five fingers." Once the host was through sharing out the mutton, he would carefully wipe his hands on his sheepskin pants. The Kyrgyz wore sheepskin in summer and winter. Sometimes I was overcome with terror when on a hot, summer day I saw a Kyrgyz man wrapped up tight in a sheepskin coat, with a shaggy hood on his head. Such clothing would serve him all day and night; Kazakh nights were most often very chilly and then sheepskin turned out to be really necessary. In the evening, after the meal, the Kyrgyz women would withdraw, while the men would sit in a ring on the floor, leaving an empty circle of bare dirt in the middle. This was time for smoking, or more often chewing, tobacco. The Kyrgyz had a special way of spitting by squirting saliva through their teeth. When they were done sitting there, the whole inside of the main room would be covered in spit.

The women often got seriously sick, but somehow

the Kyrgyz husbands were completely unconcerned about this. In fact, polygamy had been banned for a good few years, but this wasn't enforced. A wife cost a particular number of oxen and sheep. If one wife got sick, a Kyrgyz man would buy himself a new one. Her unhappy predecessor would oftentimes die slowly, lying in a corner somewhere and coughing. Most often these women were victims of TB or a difficult childbirth; they died of hemorrhages and general sepsis.

I couldn't swallow this. It was hard for me to bear this incomprehensible, cruel indifference and I felt increasingly depressed in Sadykashy.

One day a woman came to me with an advanced pregnancy. She was wearing a dress that hung down from her shoulders, but her belly was bare. Its skin was very hard and gray, scratched and flecked with scabs. I'd never seen anything like it and wondered what could have caused it. The woman explained it to me herself: she worked on a kolkhoz feeding cows; the feed was sharp, prickly steppe grass, which she scooped up by hand. First her dress got damaged and torn at the belly, so nothing could protect the skin any longer. She had no underclothes or any other dress. She worked and slept in the same one, and in that same one came to see me.

At this time I met a doctor sent to a neighboring village from the regions taken from Poland in 1939, when I was already in school in Letovochnoye. Our teachers had told us that Poland attacked the Soviet Union, but the Red Army had shown them what it was capable of. They taught us a battle song:

Chuzhoi zemli my ne khotim
No i svoyei vershka ne otdadim ...

We don't want anyone else's land,
But we won't give up an inch of ours ...

Maria, as my new acquaintance was called, told me that the head of the kolkhoz in their settlement was particularly ill-disposed to the exiles. There was no question of letting them borrow sleighs to go get food, even in the nearest villages. The Soviets had arrested Maria's husband immediately after the invasion of Poland; she had been left to her own devices with their children. They still had plenty of clothes, for which the Kyrgyz were happy to trade food, but the family had been suffering from hunger for a long time.

I had a decent relationship with my superiors in Sadykashy and I could get a sleigh on a particular day without much trouble.

We set off in calm weather for a few relatively close Kyrgyz villages. The trading went fairly easily. We stocked up a few sacks of wheat, a little flour, and clarified butter. We spent the night with some Kyrgyz and the next morning we decided to head back. Maria was anxious about the children, who'd been left unattended, and I wanted to return the horse and sleigh on time. We set off. It wasn't long before the wind whipped up. We spent half the journey sitting in the sleigh. Then the horse grew weak; it couldn't walk any further. We kept trying to feed it hay; it didn't want to eat, and the wind blew the hay from our hands. The packed-snow road was narrow.

I was standing next to the horse, but I could barely reach its mouth. We untied the sack of wheat—the animal didn't want that, either. We started encouraging it along as best we could, by pushing the sleigh. The effect was marginal; every few minutes the horse would fall down and finally it couldn't get up again. Snow kept building up, and rapidly growing snowbanks were forming around the sleigh. The snow got into every nook and cranny and threatened to bury us. Our coats had gone stiff—the cold and the blizzard were taking their toll. We'd also noticed we kept going in circles.

We were very weak, yet we knew we couldn't sit down even for a moment, because then we wouldn't get up again. We didn't even have the strength to pray. Maria was completely exhausted; she told me:

"I won't make it back now, if you survive, go see my children and tell them what happened."

Desperate, I started to shout with all the strength I had:

"Help! Help!"

After a few moments, on the trunk of a pine tree I unexpectedly saw a sign carved by the officer who'd been courting me. I kept walking and came across another sign. I hurried back to Maria.

"Get up," I said. "I know the way! Let's go!"

Maria couldn't believe it. I led her to the symbol on the pine tree—irrefutable proof that we were very near the village. We kissed that symbol, weeping with joy. We took off our coats, which were weighing us down enormously, and headed for Sadykashy. The horse, along with our acquisitions, remained in the forest, lying on its side with its legs stretched out.

By then it was dark, yet soon we saw a little light in the area of the cafeteria. We got there, falling down every few steps, although the wind had now let up. Inside we found a Jewish woman, an evacuee from Sarny who I knew well. She had two sons, Jankiel and twelve-year-old Josel, who I'd treated for typhus. She gave each of us a large portion of rich zacierki soup seasoned with butter. Jankiel, who was now seventeen, looked around to see if anyone had noticed we'd come back without the horse, and then walked us over to my apartment. He advised us not to show our faces in the village the next day, and said he and his friends would do their best to sort everything out.

Sure enough, at the crack of dawn a few volunteers set off into the forest. Another horse brought the sleigh back; as for our unfortunate animal, to this day I don't know if it was still alive or if the boys dragged home a now-ossified corpse. In the event of an investigation, I was to say that on the evening in question I brought the horse back to the stable alive and well. We hid the sacks of wheat under our beds and concealed them with a quilt that hung to the floor.

The staff in the orphanage were also on edge, because they'd let us take the horse without anyone's approval. A few days later I signed them an order saying I'd been traveling to neighboring villages, doing smallpox vaccinations. That was a reasonable cover story, but even so I wasn't sure if my "transgression" might be exposed.

Spring came, then summer, and with it a true abundance of watermelons, squashes, and tomatoes. The orphanage—the children and the staff—helped harvest them. In exchange the orphanage received a lot of land on which we planted vegetables, this time for our own use. The harvests' abundance was miraculous to me. Yet I didn't want to spend the next winter in Sadykashy. I was constantly afraid of an investigation being launched into the horse, while, secondly, I had realized something very stressful to be aware of, namely that in these conditions my medical skills were not up to scratch. We fairly frequently had difficult childbirths, where the placenta didn't want to come out or the fetus was in transverse position. Once I was forced to cut a fetus into pieces; I was terrified that that nightmarish experience might recur. I was also afraid of other difficult cases. Of course, there was no question of transportation to a hospital or contact with a doctor. Not at such great distances. In winter there was no transportation anyway.

I did, in fact, have a government ID, issued in Petropavlovsk when I was released from displaced person status, but it was only valid within Kazakhstan.

In these circumstances I started slowly thinking about how I could possibly get into the Medical Institute in Alma-Ata.

I wrote a letter of application and sent it along with my documents. The reply that came did not bode very well. Priority for study places went to war invalids, of whom by then there were very many, and their number kept rising; next in line were evacuees from Kyiv, Odesa, Kharkiv, etc. In reality I had no chance. The only possibility was to stay in Sadykashy. After reflecting, I decided to forge a new date on my komandirovka, the document allowing me to travel, and go back to Chernigovka.

At home, depression reigned. There had been no letters from Władek. My younger brother, seventeen-year-old Lucjan, had been drafted. Until this time, none of the displaced persons, at least in our area, had been called up—which had provided a certain type of peace. Yet a great deal had changed. The Soviet Union needed as much cannon fodder as possible and everyone was drafted who could be, including minors.

I told my parents about my plans. My mother cooked me a large sack of hardtack and a little pot of clarified butter. My father scraped together one thousand rubles; most of that sum he borrowed from a good friend and neighbor, Lezgin, who not only showed us generosity, but was marked by a trustworthiness rarely encountered today, in that place or in any other.

Thus equipped, I could set off. My mother decided to accompany me to Taiynsha Station. We traveled on wagons transporting wheat. It was drizzling lightly. Clay caked onto the wagon wheels. The driver covered himself with a piece of a tent, and my mother and I used an old kilim. At first it didn't let the rain through. But later, large drops of dirty water kept dripping on our faces. The oxen didn't want to move and the driver unhitched them very frequently. The sixty-kilometer journey took six days. A train passed through Taiynsha Station every other day. We had to spend the night there on a wooden bunk. At that time my mother was badly emaciated; she constantly tossed and turned, all her bones hurt.

The next day I got on a train heading for Petropavlovsk. Shortly after leaving the station, some policemen appeared and started checking documents. The officer who looked at my komandirovka noticed the date had been altered, though I thought I'd done it unnoticeably. I was led into a separate car, along with twenty other people. The police officers prepared a list of the arrestees. By my name, alongside my personal information, they wrote: *poddelka dokumentov*.[11] The other detainees, who knew a thing or two about the Soviet criminal code, declared that for something like that I was risking fifteen years in prison. It's hard to express the dread I felt on the way to Petropavlovsk.

There, under guard, we were put in a holding cell. It was a very unpleasant room: large, dark, and damp. We waited a few hours until they started summoning us one by one for questioning.

Barely able to stand, I went into an office, where sitting behind a desk was an older, maybe sixty-year-old man with the rank of major. There was no one else. After a long while I realized he was looking over my papers and, I thought … he didn't notice the forged date. Sure enough, before long he murmured a question, addressed neither to me nor to himself:

"What the heck did he want?"

"He" meant the policeman who'd arrested me.

I decided to rescue myself and said:

"My pass is from Taiynsha Station to Petropavlovsk, but I boarded one station further along, in Smirnovo."

---

11 Document forgery.

The major looked up at me, picked up the list the policeman had prepared, and crossed off my name.

"You can go," he said.

In Petropavlovsk I wanted above all to track down Lucjan. I went to the army unit. Before long the soldiers started making their way back from the training ground and I saw Lucio running toward me. He was exhausted and famished, in a frayed greatcoat with holes in it. I learned they were tormenting them with exercises from morning to night, and a whole day's food ration consisted of a bowl of watery soup, usually with only a cabbage leaf floating in it.

"They're starving us horribly here," said Lucio, "but in a few days we're meant to go to the front. I'll manage somehow, but my friend Otawczyc can't stand the hunger and keeps rifling through the trash for anything edible. Sometimes potato peelings turn up."

I can hear his words to this day and I could kick myself for not going back to the station for the hardtack. At the time, I thought my mother would come visit and bring him something. But later it turned out there wasn't time. A few days after we saw one another, Lucio got sent to the front. He often wrote to Chernigovka. The letters were short and most often read: *I'm safe and sound, in a few days, if I'm still alive, I'll write again.* But soon he was badly wounded. He spent a long time in a hospital in Smolensk. He finally got out, but with his arm completely stiff, immobilized at the elbow. Despite that he was sent once again to the front. He was killed outside Berlin on April 7, 1945.

I waited for a few days at the train station in Petropavlovsk before I managed to get on a train going to Omsk. In Omsk I had to transfer and zakompa-sirovat' my ticket: this was something like a reservation, and was required—without it a ticket was invalid. But the ticket office wasn't doing validations. People waited entire days. A woman walked around the station with a little bell and announced that on such-and-such a train there were no open spaces and there would be no reservations. There weren't many benches, almost all the travelers were camped out on their bundles.

Finally I made it to Novosibirsk.

What happened in Omsk was a walk in the park compared to the hell in which I found myself at Novosibirsk Station. Travelers had been waiting there for whole weeks. New ones kept arriving, but no one was managing to leave. Naturally, trains frequently rolled through the station, but no one was let onto the platforms. I started wondering if it would make more sense to stay in Novosibirsk. They also had a Medical Institute there, but getting through the winter required pimy, which cost a thousand rubles. So all the money I had I would spend on felt boots. Meanwhile, in Alma-Ata that sum would be enough to pay for bread rations for an entire year.[12]

My quandary ended one night when thieves cut open my bag and stole my thousand rubles. Now, one way or the other I couldn't stay in Novosibirsk. After two weeks of waiting I learned that there was a prisoner train on a sidetrack and if I somehow bribed a guard, he'd let me into one of the cars.

---

12 At the time a rationed kilo of bread cost seventy rubles; on the open market, the same bread would cost from five hundred to seven hundred rubles.

I went to the market and sold my little pot of butter. I got eight hundred rubles for it. In Novosibirsk there were a large number of people evacuated from the battlefields; a great proportion of them were Jews. They had a lot of money and would stock up on food at the market. Selling the butter didn't present any difficulties.

I bribed the guard and found myself in a car full of Uzbek prisoners. They were not—it turned out—criminal prisoners, guilty of theft, rape, or murder. They had none of the predatory mentality of the bezprizornye,[13] the zaklyuchonnye,[14] or recidivists. They had been imprisoned for passive resistance to the obligatory habits and duties of the Soviet citizen. They were friendly to me, helpful—very, as they say in Poland, "w porządku." They were also incredibly derelict, louse-infested, and dirty. The Soviet government was treating them brutally. It had no use for them at the front, nor could it coerce them into forced labor at the so-called trudovoi front[15] in mines or arms factories, often in the open air, in terrible cold.

The train kept getting sent off onto sidings, where we'd wait for a few days. The journey was torment. It lasted seventeen days.

---

13 Aggressive, care-deprived youths.
14 Gulag prisoners.
15 Labor front.

ALMA-ATA

When I finally reached my destination, Alma-Ata seemed like a miracle.

On either side of the paved streets floated aryki, little brooks of lovely-tasting spring water, intended to irrigate the ground and the numerous gardens here. I washed my face in the aryki and paddled my feet. I felt fatigue subsiding and my strength coming back. I thought the water from these little springs had miraculous, healing powers.

The city was overflowing with greenery, the fruit stands were heaped up with piles of colorful apples, watermelons, peaches, apricots. You could encounter beautifully dressed women in the company of elegant men. Posters on walls announced the opera house was showing *Rusalka* by Dvořák. Later I learned that many artists had been evacuated here from Moscow, including Zhdanov, Orlova, and Nazvanova; you could sometimes run into them strolling in the streets.

Yet the other neighborhoods of Alma-Ata, a little ways away from downtown, were different. There you'd often see Uzbeks lying in the street, dying of hunger. No social services cared for them, and the police, when summoned, would say:

"Chort s nim, ne khochet voyevat', pust' podokhnet."[16]

My journey lasted so long that I was late for the entrance exams. It couldn't have been clearer that they wouldn't accept me into the program. Still, I thought that maybe I'd be able to get a job somewhere in a

---

16 The hell with him, he doesn't want to fight—he can croak.

hospital. Meanwhile, to make myself somehow at home in this new place, I hurried straight to the Medical Institute, wanting at least to see what it looked like.

A huge number of young women were wandering the halls.

In the Soviet Union women were now being taken into the military as well. Because medical students were exempt, many young women took advantage of this to avoid the draft. There weren't many Kazakh girls; you could recognize them by their distinctive facial features, raven-black hair, and their complexions, which were dark though not as yellow as that of the Kyrgyz women. They all wore little suits of crushed plush in garish colors: yellow, red, raspberry, violet.

Young women evacuated from the war zones made up the clear majority of students. Both the Kazakhs and I observed them with interest. They had dresses in all sorts of cuts, pleated, flouncy, made of a range of fabrics. They often wore high-heeled pumps, usually badly scuffed; many also had knee-high winter boots made of badly dirtied suede, also with high heels. Most eye-catching of all was their makeup: a thick layer of powder and garish lipstick, which left little streams running down the corners of their mouths; eyebrows shaved off and redrawn in black pencil. It was also clearly considered elegant to put brown "beauty marks" on the lower part of their face.

From conversations in the hallways I learned some things that seemed very intriguing. The evacuees often had no documents; usually they had to be taken at their word, especially when they insisted that bombs had blown all their possessions to pieces, and they themselves had barely escaped with their lives. I'm sure this was often true; but more often such stories were invented for the purposes of the moment. One of the girls, looking brave and resolute, said openly that while her sister had, of course, gone to college, she herself hadn't really; yet she'd registered here as a third-year, because before it came out that she didn't know how to do anything, the war would surely be over.

The line to reception was very long. Just in case, I decided to join it. I felt a faint spark of hope that maybe, I might just ... The closer I got to the window, the more worried I was. I was seized by a paralyzing sense of helplessness, but also a fierce yearning to achieve my goal, or at least get closer to it. It was so strong that I stood there pulled every which way, feeling the contradictions very acutely. I wanted to pray, but I couldn't put together a single, even short prayer.

Finally, somewhat unexpectedly because the young woman in front of me was dealt with quickly, I found myself in front of the window.

My hands trembling, I handed over my papers: my government ID, my feldsher school diploma, my work certificate.

I heard the question: "Vy Pol'ka?"

"Yes," I replied. "I'm Polish."

"I always got the impression," said the woman receiving us on the other side of the window, who looked to be forty or forty-five, with a beautiful though tired face, probably a secretary, "that all Polish women had blue eyes and blonde hair. But your hair is black ..."

At the same time she was flipping through the pages in her admission book.

"Ah, here we go!" I hear her voice from very far away. "Waśkowska, Franceska, daughter of Stefan, born in 1923, Polish. You've been accepted into the medical faculty. You've been assigned to the residential program. I'll just give you your referral for the dormitory."

I was dumbfounded. As if in a dream, I collected my papers. I turned away from the window. I walked down the halls, passing groups of young women. I ended up outside. To this day I don't know, I don't understand, what really happened then. I was walking faster and faster. I felt the overwhelming need to thank God for such huge, such unexpected luck. I stopped by a stream. My gratitude was so great that none of the prayers I knew could express it. What I felt was my heart's most passionate action.

I finally somehow regained my composure. Once again I reflected on my situation.

The Medical Institute had three faculties operating: medical, pediatric, and sanitary-epidemiological. The medical faculty was the hardest to get into. Nor did many get a spot in the dorm. I had both. This surprising gift of fate inspired an internal conviction that Providence was watching over me and its care was what had made all this happen. Just as when I got my displacement status lifted and when I was accepted into feldsher school, the hope returned that my life might move toward a brighter future. That maybe I would someday be able to escape the vicious circle.

The dormitory was a grand building with a beautiful, large lobby hung with mirrors. Stairs led to the upper floors, which held three- or four-person rooms assigned to third-, fourth- and fifth-year students. I was meant to live on the ground floor in a twenty-person room. This was a vast space with eleven beds, each one shared between two students. My sleeping companion was a Russian with pale skin and blonde hair. The other twenty girls were Jewish.

A washroom with two faucets was located at the end of the corridor, while there was always a long line for the toilets. From somewhere my roommates got a bucket that we could pee into in peace. We put together a roster of who was meant to take it out, and when. But the girls, future doctors, somehow didn't mind dumping out the bucket's contents onto the floor—there it would dry up easily, making its presence known with a familiar stench.

The cafeteria was downstairs. There, once per day, we could get a mug of soup. To do so, we had to clip out of our ration cards the appropriate twenty grams of semolina. Both the head of the kitchen and the cook must—of course—have siphoned off a little of that quantity. As a result the pot was most often full of slightly cloudy hot water, with barely a trace amount of grain floating in it.

A group photo of students at the Medical Institute in
Alma-Ata; the author is the first on the right in the top row.

There were six hundred students in the first year.
They split us into two groups of three hundred each.
One group had lectures in the morning, the other in
the afternoon. The lectures really were all right, and
often interestingly given; to this day, looking back
years later, I consider them high quality and satis-
fying.

But there was something that kept us from making the most of them: hunger's increasingly strong
grip on our throats.

Everyone would get four hundred grams of bread
a day. Apart from that, we could only drink that
translucent soup, more like cloudy water that was
hard to call food.

To make matters worse, the bread was very heavy.
Amid widespread pilfering, the bakers had to add
something to the flour to make the little loaf pan

weigh 1,200 grams. The saleswomen didn't always divide the loaf evenly into three parts, and one of those portions was someone's food for a whole day.

Soon we were famished to the point we couldn't sleep at night. We were tormented by hunger cramps and stomachaches. We would wait for dawn, so at five in the morning we could go to the store and buy our daily ration (which cost, I believe, fifty kopecks). Most often we ate it right away. Later we'd think: "Why didn't I leave myself even a little piece; if I could swallow even just a bite now, that would make it easier." Then again, the times when, with a great effort of will, you did actually leave a bit for later, all day long it was impossible to think of anything else, let alone focus on the lectures.

Each week got worse and worse. The lecturers were going hungry too. Our Latin professor told us how to make the bread last longer. He was a very good man who was often taken advantage of or mocked.

"Today, for instance," he would say, "I haven't eaten any bread and I've got nothing left on my ration card. The saleslady gave me three days of rations, but I've got nothing, I just don't know if I ate it or if someone stole it from me."

This man clearly had nowhere he could go, because he slept in the lecture hall, in the last row at the top. He carried a little shopping bag with him, which held an empty food can that he used as a mug, and a little piece of bread, with which he would demonstrate to us how much he would eat, how much he would leave himself, and how long it needed to last. He went around in a frayed overcoat, which sometimes had strips of torn lining dragging after it or pieces of padding hanging from it. Sometimes jokers would sneak up behind him and step on these dragging shreds. He was an enthusiast for classical culture and the Latin language. I remember a lesson in which he delighted in the sound of the noun *chamomilla* (chamomile); he savored repeating the word several times.

The director of the institute didn't notice—or rather didn't want to notice—the Latin professor's situation. The director was named Zyuzin. He was a well-built man, and even better fed and dressed. He often wore white jackets and we'd usually see him in the company of various women. Rumor had it they were all his lovers. In addition he was a very active party official and mainly dealt with so-called social issues. One such issue would come to torment us.

All the students, nearly all of whom were women, were forced to do hard labor, excavating at a construction site for an electric plant. This happened a few times a week, and always on Sunday at that. There were no excavators, so we dug with nothing but shovels. We had to carry the dirt out in wheelbarrows up a narrow, winding path. It was work well beyond our strength—the strength, when all is said and done, of starving young women. We weren't given anything to drink, much less to eat. People were constantly passing out.

When this forced labor began, our Jewish friends found a method that on a few occasions let them avoid this hell. Namely, they got hold of the key to our room; when the Komsomol'tsy—members of the Communist Youth League—came to herd us out to the excavation site, the Jewish girls would lock themselves in and hide on the floor under the beds. When the Komsomol'tsy peeked through the window and the keyhole, there was no one in sight. It couldn't last long—the Komsomol'tsy got hold of keys for all the rooms and our conspiracy wasn't much use anymore.

These living conditions exhausted me completely—physically and mentally. I felt that I had to look for some way out, because I couldn't bear it any longer.

It was 1944. Loudspeakers on the streets were blaring nonstop. They announced triumphantly that the German military was retreating and the Red Army had just liberated Ukraine. They exhorted people to return to the recovered regions and rebuild the destroyed cities.

I went to the dean's office and asked to transfer to another university. I had no difficulty doing so. Alma-Ata was overpopulated and so far no one was volunteering to return. They wrote me up a transfer to Voronezh.

HOME AGAIN

Summer vacation began and I immediately decided to go to Chernigovka. I missed my parents badly, and I also wanted to find out whether there was any news from my brothers, and how my sister was doing. Educated by experience, I sewed my 150-ruble fortune into my underwear and set off on a long, difficult journey. Finally I got to Taiynsha Station.

I knew some people there who would put me up for the night; they gladly took me in and offered me dinner. Large white potatoes were cooking in a little can placed in the bread oven, and their tops were toasting to a golden color, giving off an aroma I found utterly heavenly. My hostess took the potatoes out and poured them into a large bowl on the table. I never again laid eyes on a more marvelous still-life, nor one so fragrant. A few potatoes fell out of the bowl and rolled along the bright, white-scrubbed boards.

The whole year in Alma-Ata I hadn't seen a single potato. I wanted to keep my composure, but it didn't really work. I kept reaching for another potato, promising myself this one would be the last. After dinner my hostess's husband left to find out if a wagon was heading toward Chernigovka in the next few days; the woman busied herself cleaning, and I kept secretly reaching into the bowl.

In the morning I got on a wagon going toward Letovochnoye. That wasn't the shortest route, but I preferred moving to waiting. The driver was in no hurry; twice he unhitched the oxen so they could graze a little. I took advantage of the occasion to slip my hand into his bag, full of crumbs of white wheat bread, for a secret snack.

In the evening we reached Letovochnoye. I went

straight to the Marchlewskis', where I'd lodged for two years. Pani Marchlewska took me in very generously, and when she placed some white cheese coated in sour cream in front of me, I couldn't have been happier.

The next afternoon I reached Chernigovka. The whole way, since morning, I'd had one thing on my mind: did my family have anything to eat, were they getting by, or were they starving instead? I pictured the moment when I'd enter the house. *I'm sure*, I thought, *I'll be able to tell right away how things are going, whether they've got anything or nothing to eat.*

Sure enough, it only took the first few seconds: on the kitchen hutch I saw a large loaf of bread; next to it, on a wooden bench, a bowl full of cold potatoes; and in a pot on the stove—some type of soup.

We were overjoyed to see one another. I was no less glad that I wouldn't have to go hungry anymore. My mother got straight to molding sweet cheese pierogies, and there was also some kind of mutton stew and as much bread as I could eat. I ate nonstop, with my mother constantly placing new servings in front of me. She finally started worrying a little.

"Maybe don't eat any more," she said. "You might get sick."

But I just kept on eating.

In the middle of the night, powerful hunger awoke me again. I heard my mother whispering to my father:

"Why did I let her eat so much … She can't sleep, her stomach hurts."

"I'm not sick," I replied, "just hungry; give me something to eat."

My mother couldn't find kerosene for the lamp, but I managed perfectly well in the dark. I found the bread and pierogies and ate again.

The next day the neighbor ladies came over. After giving my haggard figure a looking-over, they declared I had TB and my days were surely numbered. They told the story of a young girl, Kudymowska, who had recently died of galloping consumption. They also mentioned my older friend Helenka Stelmach, who most likely had TB of the bone. Her knee joints were swollen, misshapen, red-and-dark-blue. Pus oozed from fistulas. Soon the disease also attacked her hip joints. Helenka, the same girl who at school in Marachivka refused a couple kluski for herself so she could take them to her starving mother, now herself was very sick and suffering badly. She couldn't walk. Before she died, she lay motionless for an entire year.

As for me, I didn't feel sick. My father said:

"Some consumption, she's eating enough for three harvestmen!"

My parents bought a sheep, so I had some meat too; they also told me to drink suet and dog fat. I didn't do that, but my mother did pour the suet over potatoes, and fry potato pancakes and blinis in it.

Almost everyone in Chernigovka now had a cow of their own. From time to time they would buy a sheep from the Kazakhs, and once in a while they'd steal a calf from the kolkhoz. Several families would divide the meat among themselves. When the theft was discovered the following day, there'd be no way to prove anything against anyone, since everything would get eaten up right away.

Every now and then a judge would turn up. When I got back to Chernigovka, he was in the midst of fulfilling the local demand for justice. He set up a table and chair under the open sky and in this setting, outdoors, trials were held. I went to see what illicit behavior was going on in our settlement.

The judge was just hearing an accusation from Tekla Wysocka. She'd allegedly had a romance with the husband of Netykszyna, who took revenge on her rival by filling a bucket with waste from an outhouse pit and dumping it on her head. The judge ruled that for her deed, Netykszyna would pay a five-ruble fine.

The woman put a ten-ruble bill on the table. The judge was confused.

"I don't have any change," he said.

"No need," replied Netykszyna. "I'm gonna dump that slut again."

General merriment broke out. Even the judge audibly snickered.

I felt something strange was going on. For a good little while I couldn't work out what was so odd. Finally I put my finger on it: our villagers were laughing out loud!

Summer vacation was spent in preparations for my departure. But my plans changed somewhat. Over the radio receiver we heard news that the Red Army had liberated Kharkiv. The previously evacuated population, especially young people, were called on to return to their ruined city. Words of encouragement were spoken: apparently the rubble was already partially cleared, one streetcar was running and … a Medical Institute was opening up. *Why*, I thought, *Kharkiv is already Ukraine! That means I'm moving west, closer and closer to Poland. Since they're encouraging us so much on the radio, maybe they'd let me study there?*

That thought kept niggling at me. I had been living in Kazakhstan since the age of thirteen. From my childhood I remembered vividly the lush vegetation of Ukraine, the pitch-black earth and the splendid, towering forests. Meanwhile, in Kazakhstan everything was gray-gold-dun and monotonous as the local steppe. The eternally wind-blown, sharp, and always dry grass known as kovyl and the barrel-shaped bunches of steppe weeds rolling nowhere, blown by the wind, exuded nothing but sadness. I only had to think of the abundant Ukrainian landscape and my heart would fill with hope and the longing to return.

At home we started drying bread for hardtack. It was right in the middle of the harvest. Marysia had to work once again as a tractor driver. The so-called encampment—meaning the tractors and combine harvesters—was located eight kilometers from the village. The people working there weren't able to return home for the night. Work began at first light and ended at dusk. Going home would be dangerous anyway, because of wolves. The harvesters therefore had to abandon their village and loved ones for a good several months. Harvests in Kazakhstan went on a very long time, until October or November, and even longer if there was no snow. Frost didn't hinder the reaping; the grain and straw stayed dry. Rain in this climate was a rarity. There was no morning dew, either.

I visited Marysia almost every day. Those almost-barracks of hers, on the grounds of the encampment, had something like a kitchen where the cook, day in and day out, made the same dish: kluski in water. It attracted such a quantity of flies that the woman struggled to move among them; she was even hard to see. I called her outside to find out where my sister was working that day. Inside it was impossible to talk because the insects were buzzing too loudly; it was dangerous even to open your mouth. It sounds unlikely but it's true. Once I knew where Marysia was working I walked another few kilometers to see her.

My sister, once she was through the first bout of illness, had to go back to work that was just as hard as before. Almost exclusively women worked the harvest; most men had been sent off to war. In the encampment, apart from the kitchen, there was also a wall built of mudbrick, against which stood bunks made of hammered planks. The women were reluctant to lie down on them for the night, because there were a lot of ticks in that spot. Most often they just slept on the steppe, on top of a quilted jacket or an overcoat. Nonetheless they were amply supplied with bread. On my way from the encampment back to Chernigovka, I would always bring two or three loaves with me; I'd slice them into a few pieces and before I got home the steppe wind would have dried the bread into hardtack.

The threshed grain was poured out into huge mounds stretching dozens of meters. From there, oxcarts would transport it to Taiynsha railroad station. A one-way journey took five days. So the grain lay in the mounds for a very long time. A small number of men, such as remained, were assigned to guard this open-air silo.

The task seemed pointless; it was hard to steal a whole sack because no one could heft it all the way back to the village, and everyone took small amounts, for instance to use as chicken feed. Much grain went to waste. It got left on the ground, in the grass, or it blew away in the wind. Yet the local authorities had resolved that at night the harvest had to be guarded. Every few days it was my father's turn. He'd dress in a sheepskin coat, because Kazakh nights were always cool, and for fear of wolves he'd arrive at his destination well before sunset. He'd walk among the mounds for a while, then later make a place to sleep on one of them.

One of these nights something happened to him that would be hard to believe if my father weren't a levelheaded man certain to be absolutely bereft of any tendency to fantasize—so the story he told us definitely happened.

Dawn was just approaching when he was awakened feeling short of breath and with some kind of weight on his chest. Before he opened his eyes, he could tell a large living creature was lying on top of him. He placed his left hand on it and felt fur beneath his fingers, and then by touch he recognized a paw. Now he knew it was a wolf; he could hear the sleeping intruder's measured breathing. He was seized with terror. He was afraid his heartbeat and fear-accelerated breathing would awaken the wolf.

He decided to conquer his fright and prepare to defend himself. He held his hands at the ready to grab the animal by the neck or the muzzle; at the same time he slowly did his best to slip out from under the predator. The fact he was lying on loose grain made this easier. After a while only a paw remained on my father's body. He lifted it up as gently as he could, but right at that moment he felt a tail wave. The sky had grown light enough that he could see the animal in all its glory. He slowly slid further and further away, carefully crossed himself, stood up, and very slowly started walking away from the wolf. He was expecting that at any moment he might feel its fangs on his throat. He didn't know if the animal had woken up or was still sleeping. As the distance between them grew, he quickened his pace. He headed toward the encampment. Finally he decided to look behind him. The wolf was no longer asleep. It was standing and looking right at its sleeping companion. Maybe it was weighing up its chances? It surely could tell it was alone—and wolves apparently attack in packs. Sometimes small ones, but packs nonetheless. Especially when they come across such large prey as a human. After a moment, the wolf stretched lazily, yawned, and took a few steps. It lifted its back paw, peed on a little bulge on the mound and set off in the opposite direction.

From that time on no one went alone to guard the grain, and we thanked God that our father had made it home safe and sound.

Meanwhile I had now gathered up a lot of hardtack. I used querns to make it into flour, because in that form food supplies were much easier to transport. The sack really was heavy, but on the other hand more convenient in difficult situations at the station or on the train. After all, there were no platforms anywhere. Getting into a train car took no small effort, much less if you had a sack of hardtack on your back, sticking out and bumping into everything. An acrobat would barely be able to manage. At the stations you could get kipyatok, meaning hot, boiled water. I would pour a little flour into it and I'd have something warm and nourishing to eat.

When I got to Taiynsha Station, it turned out the train had just left. The next wouldn't arrive for two days. I suppose all the train cars running at the time were designated for military purposes, only incidentally picking up passengers. There were, of course, no passenger cars.

I spent several days of my journey on a flatcar with some military equipment. I was already very tired from riding in the wind, without a roof over my head, when at one station I managed to shove my way onto a car full of people. I don't know how I did it, since there was an indescribable crush. People were standing pressed against one another; if you picked up one foot to shift your bodyweight, there would be no space left to put it down again.

Standing near me was a girl who looked to be from the Caucasus, with a plump little sack of dried peaches—known there as uryuk—on her shoulder. She was riding from Tashkent. She knew that at some station further along a few people from our car were meant to get off.

"We have to push in that direction," she taught me.

She was right; it got a little looser, though not enough to sit on the floor. But it was still a great relief.

I rode like that all the way to Kharkiv.

KHARKIV

When I got off the train, I found myself surrounded by pockmarked ruins and heaps of rubble. Everything was covered in heavy, black dust. Stumps of ruined buildings stretched as far as the eye could see. By the train tracks there was nothing you could call a station or waiting room. Night was approaching and the people who'd disembarked were afraid to spend it out in the open. We'd heard stories—since meeting in the car, the girl from Tashkent and I had stuck together—that there was a gang called "the Black Cat" prowling the city. They were allegedly ruthless bandits, unyielding in pursuit of a few rubles' worth of loot or some better wardrobe item. So we walked straight ahead, keeping an eye out for human residences in the rubble. We were turned away everywhere we asked for accommodation. All the surviving apartments were overcrowded; often, more than a dozen people were camped out in one room. Someone suggested we seek out the kvartalnyi, the district police chief; maybe he would point us to a roof over our heads or at least tell us where to spend the night. So we kept walking along the street, which was mainly cleared of rubble, and asking passersby for his address. Then a woman came up to us and whispered a question in Yiddish. I gathered she was asking if we were Jewish. Without a second thought, I answered yes.

The woman took us to her apartment. It was a spacious room with two little children romping around. She asked us to look after them while she went out to get milk. She was gone a long time. We were worried what would happen once it came out that we weren't Jewish—after all, we knew neither the language nor the customs. Wouldn't she kick us out of the house? When she returned, we owned up that we didn't speak Yiddish. But she waved this off and said that actually she didn't either. The weight lifted from our hearts. Together we ate a little hard-tack flour and some dried peaches. The woman made us a makeshift bed on the floor and hunted down a little bundle to rest our heads on. In the morning we thanked her for putting us up and we all went our separate ways.

I wanted as soon as possible to locate the university for which I'd chosen this desperate journey. Before the war there had been three medical schools in Kharkiv, now they'd been combined into one. I was sent to a dormitory known as the Giant. It was a many-storied building that by some miracle had escaped the bombs. The walls had survived untouched, but apart from them there was nothing. Literally—nothing. The windows and doors had been partly blown out in air raids, while the locals had long since used up the remaining ones for fuel. The ground floor went to students who were war invalids. Most of them were on crutches; almost all of them were missing an arm or a leg; some had even lost their sight. The next few floors were taken up by students from a variety of programs and schools. There the rooms were also furnished to some extent. I and seven other applicants were assigned a room on the eighth floor.

We started our new life—and the next phase of our studies—by retrieving a door from the rubble and searching in the ruins for beds. Several times we found doors that seemed appropriate; once we'd finally dragged them to the eighth floor, it would turn out they didn't fit, and our hard labor had gone to waste. Finally we dug out some that we could get into the frames. I also found a bed. One without bedcords, it was true, but I rigged up a substitute using wire, with the result that I often landed on the floor.

Our room had two large openings where windows had been. We were ordered to brick one up completely, and the other by two-thirds. The remaining one-third was meant to be glazed. This would make the room fairly dim. It wasn't hard to get bricks and clay. We ran up and down the stairs with our "construction material" and soon—our experience growing, our expertise growing—we polished off all the bricklaying. At that time we didn't yet feel the torment of the eighth floor. Only after a while, when we each had to carry several buckets of water up and down a few times a day, did we feel, each of us, how tough it was. November was long gone and there was still no glass. We covered the unbricked part of the window with rags. Yet each time someone opened the door a draft kicked up that blew away that safety barrier.

Winter came, and with it, powerful cold. There was no functioning heat in our dorm. We were absolutely freezing. One day one of our friends went to visit her mother. She brought back with her a large cast-iron canister with the bottom worn through from long use. We scavenged sheet metal pipes, bricks, and clay from the ruins. Out of all of these items we built a stove, whose smoke was directed outside through the pipes. This construction improved our situation greatly. We could even put a pot on this setup and in a few minutes, presto, we'd have warm water. Even better: we could cook something too! Yet soon worse cold arrived; it was now only warm right next to the stove, and when we used it to wash our hair, before one of us could brush it out, little icicles would have formed at the ends. Of course there was no electricity. Next to our beds we had lamps we'd built ourselves. They were made of bottles of gasoline, slices of potatoes, and pieces of bandage replacing the wick. These were the oil lamps we would study by at night. We had dark rings on our faces around our noses and mouths. In the morning, we'd cough and spit black saliva all the way to class, as was particularly visible on the white snow.

The lecture hall and classrooms were in a no less lamentable state. There were holes all over the walls and floors, which meant rats took a particular liking to these rooms.

Once during a lecture, one of the girls suddenly leapt up with a strange yelp and sped out into the hall. She had an uncanny look in her eyes and a face white as a sheet; after a moment she went silent and for a long time she couldn't utter a word; she was in shock. Everyone thought it was a case of sudden hysteria.

"You see," said the assistant leading the class, "this is one way the horrible experiences we've had in wartime can affect our psychological health."

Meanwhile it turned out the cause of her alleged insanity was a rat. The girl hadn't felt it climbing up her leg because she was wearing thick stockings; only when it got under her skirt, above the stockings, did she leap up, terrified, stamping, jumping—and also screaming—to rid herself of the intruder.

Our daily schedule included other "diversions"— though they were more dangerous.

A politruk[17] was now operating at the university. Almost every day someone was called out of a lecture for, as it was called, a "dopros."[18] Particularly susceptible were students who during the German occupation had not been either evacuated or deported by the Germans for labor. The politruk didn't believe their families had hidden them and he used every possible means to make them admit they'd collaborated with the Germans.

From the very beginning I presented myself as someone evacuated to Kazakhstan only after the start of the war; I never let on that my family had been deported in 1936. This got me out of the interrogations. But there were girls who, after one or several such questionings, never came back to class. I remember the mother of one of my friends; she came to school many days in a row to find out what had happened to her daughter. She was always waiting outside the office of the politruk, who had no desire to speak to her. Finally one day he replied he had no idea where her daughter might be. "I'm sure she's home," he said. "Anyway, you're the one who should know where she is."

---

17 A political officer, a representative of the NKVD.
18 Interrogation.

The fifth semester of school passed.

Here the hunger was not so nagging as in Kazakhstan, in Alma-Ata or even earlier, home in Ukraine. We could buy cornmeal, which we'd heat with water or milk; fairly often we'd get potatoes. What made our lives most repugnant were the living conditions: bitter cold in the rooms, dirt, rats, soot getting into every nook and cranny. The soot would stubbornly clog the pipes of our little stove, and then smoke would fill up the room and sting our eyes. We did our best to clean it out very carefully, but most often it would pour out all over the room or on the stairs, and before long it was everywhere: on the floor, in our clothes chests, in our ears. Luckily I had an overcoat made of black plush; wonder of wonders, it looked all right, even though I both slept and cleaned the stove in it.

Another inconvenience was the total lack of paper. The only paper goods available on the market at that time were books by Comrade Stalin, sold fairly cheaply at kiosks. Of necessity they served every purpose that paper normally did. Soon we found the gaps between the lines of text were wide enough to take lecture notes in them. We wrote with copying pencils. Using a fountain pen was impossible because of the awful quality of the paper, while pencils usually weren't suitable either, because by our makeshift lamps—even if you had the best eyesight—there was no way to read the notes you'd made.

But most maddening of all turned out to be the lack of soap. In Kazakhstan we'd known how to make it ourselves, out of animal fat, eggs, and caustic soda. But here, there were no cleaning products—apart from water. Yet when it came to getting rid of soot, just water was unfortunately not enough.

Some new clothes, or even fabric, were beyond our wildest dreams. Hence we were all profoundly amazed when one of our friends turned up in a new dress. She also had a scrap of fabric with her. It was wonderful material, strong, falling beautifully, with a nice, soothing, dark green color.

"Where did you get that? Is someone selling it? Can we still get some?" We bombarded her with questions.

It turned out someone had found the fabric in the woods, up a tree.

Kharkiv: Soviet soldiers during the battle against the German Army for the city.

Before long, its owner bitterly regretted getting the chance to make that dress. It unexpectedly caused considerable problems. Namely, the NKVD—alert as ever to all kinds of threats, active as pointer dogs tracking game—launched a deep investigation into the matter on a huge, almost national scale. The young woman was interrogated nonstop. They suspected she'd been concealing—or maybe even still was concealing—some paratrooper. I think over a dozen times she had to point out the pine tree in the forest where the unfortunate rag had been hanging. The dress was—of course—confiscated. They had to test what country the material had come from, as well as many other important details—indeed, it was a matter of the security of the whole Soviet Union. Of the meaning and essence of tomorrow …

More or less at this time, news went around that the Soviet military, consumed with its mission of liberating the world, had captured the Romanian city of Chernivtsi.[19] Its indigenous inhabitants, especially the young people, were fleeing into the interior of the country, not yet taken by the Soviets. Meanwhile a Soviet administration had been installed in the city. Among other things, it was decided to organize a Medical Institute there, where they intended to

---

19   From 1918 to 1940, the city belonged to Romania, as Cernăuți. In summer of 1940 it was annexed to the Soviet Union under the Russian name Chernovitsy. After the German occupation this was changed to Chernovtsy in Russian, or Chernivtsi in Ukrainian. It is situated in southwestern Ukraine.

immediately launch all five years of a medical program, as if there were nothing more important going on in the city. The Institute was supposed to keep operating, operating "normally." Evidently there were orders to send thirty students per year of study from Kharkiv, Kyiv, and Odesa to Chernivtsi, and to start classes in the second half of the year. I found this a little bizarre. Kharkiv had only the meagre remains of three medical schools, but in Chernivtsi right off the bat a whole university was meant to get up and running? Yet we were used to any conceivable ridiculousness, with every step, with every day—as experienced citizens of the Soviet Union, we were prepared for anything. Only those who were truly determined to study and change something in their lives overcame the difficulties, obstacles, and absurdities.

For instance, in our anatomic pathology class, there was only one microscope. To know how to distinguish diseased from healthy tissue, you needed, above all, to firmly memorize what healthy kidney, liver, or lung parenchyma look like. So we'd all line up for that single microscope of ours.

"Look, here's normal lung tissue, and this is red hepatization, which occurs in the first phase of pneumonia," the teaching assistant would say, while simultaneously a newly enlightened young man or woman would be pushed to the back and unceremoniously hurried along.

Even so, the teaching assistant was a truly conscientious and generous woman and genuinely wanted us to learn her subject. As long as the next group didn't storm the door, her classes would always run long, and she'd patiently hear out all questions and resolve any doubts. If we were missing a particular preparation, she would draw it in chalk on the board. I don't remember her name, but I remember her face very well. She suffered from cutaneous TB; she no longer had skin surrounding her nostrils, just a red bridge sticking out.

One evening we were sitting around our stove. That day it wasn't giving off too much heat, because we couldn't get the wet wood to burn. We had already long ago gathered everything from the surrounding ruins that might feed the fire. Ash was spilling out around the stove. None of us had the strength to start cleaning.

"Tomorrow I'll go to the dean's office and ask if we really can go to Chernivtsi," I said suddenly, surprising even myself.

"Sounds like you want to pack your bags for prison," replied one of the girls. "I mean, the politruk sits in the dean's office all day just sniffing around for someone to work on."

"I think you should go," said another. "In prison you'll probably have a window, and here we've been waiting for glass since November. And now it's February. I guess we'll brick up the rest of the window hole; sure, it'll be dark, but it'll be the end of these miserable drafts."

The next day, my heart pounding, I walked into the dean's office. The politruk wasn't there, and the dean immediately confirmed the news about Chernivtsi. Her secretary only asked if I'd passed my exams and had my classes credited for the fifth semester.

"We're treating this matter as urgent," she said. "Classes are starting before the end of February."

I went out onto the street. Again, just like back then in Alma-Ata, I had the feeling that Providence was very clearly lending me its hand. I walked down the rubble-cleared streets of the city until I saw an Orthodox church in front of me. It was open. Inside they were holding a service. Most of the believers were men in military overcoats. Almost all on crutches, without legs or arms. Some had wooden "prostheses," others used belts to hold up their raised pant legs. Sleeves, sometimes one, sometimes the other, were tucked into pockets. Their faces, exhausted and pale, reflected the suffering they'd had to go through. Death had surely looked them in the eye more than once and left a deep mark on them. But they were alive and thanking God for their lives, their greatest treasure. Their eyes shone in haggard faces—shone with the glow of bitterness, but also of life and of gratitude.

I spent a long time in front of the altar. I was happy. I felt faith inside and was attempting to give it shape.

I think that was the first time in my life I'd gone into a church consciously, for the sake of my heart's needs. The church in Kharkiv had been opened by the Germans and the authorities had clearly not gotten around to closing it again.

I thought back to my distant relationship with the Church in childhood.

In 1930 or 1931, back before the Great Famine in Ukraine, one day my parents and I had found ourselves in Berezdiv. There was only one subject on the entire village's lips: today the last Mass would be held; the next day the Catholic parish would cease to exist. The priest would depart and there would be no Holy Sacrament in the church. It would be turned into some kind of storehouse or club.

Credit for the fifth semester of studies at the Medical Faculty of Kharkiv Medical Institute.

Then my parents and grandmother made a quick decision: I needed to have my First Communion. I generally knew my catechism, because my mother had been preparing me at home; I'd learn the rest later—that's what she told the priest.

We headed for the church. I was wearing a new red dress. On the way my grandmother's neighbor caught up to us, holding her granddaughter's dress in her hand—it had red flowers, but on a white background.

"At least there'll be a little white," she said.

We took off my new dress and put on the other one, with the white background.

The church was mobbed. A confessional had been set up in the courtyard. I was pushed with great difficulty through the packed human mass. No one wanted to give way or let someone skip in front of them. I found it hard to breathe amid the sweaty men.

That day I went to my first confession and communion.

Then came famine, exile, and Kazakhstan. I'd never been inside a church again. I knew that December 25 was Christmas. My mother had written to me about Easter in letters: *Don't work that day, because it will be Easter.* Apart from that I'd actually had no opportunity for religious practice. But I did have faith in God and trust that He was watching over us. In these especially trying circumstances, with ever greater complications all around us and serious dangers starting to threaten, I instinctively turned toward the Almighty. I asked for help, and help came. Often in such cases the most difficult issues resolved themselves, and the dangers somehow receded—sometimes at the last minute.

Guided by this joyful feeling, I went back to the dean's office. I couldn't even get a request in before the secretary handed me a transcript. It was a double-sided piece of paper pulled out of a notebook, affixed with my photograph and a list of exams I'd passed, with stamps and my professors' signatures. This was called a zachotnaya knizhka. The path to Chernivtsi was open.

CHERNIVTSI

In Chernivtsi, before I'd even left the train station, I could feel another reality surrounding me. I could see I'd arrived in a different world, a world of order.

This happened right away thanks to ... the steps from the train car to the platform. For the first time in my travels I didn't have to jump from a height of about 1.5 meters to get off the train. If I'd had to embark, I could have gone up the steps, holding the handrail, instead of, as always before, performing difficult acrobatic and often collective maneuvers for my foot to reach the floor of the car, with the mandatory sack of hardtack on my back always causing additional problems. Meanwhile here, in Chernivtsi, I simply disembarked. I was sorely tempted to get back on and get right off again. But all the passengers were leaving the station, so I hurried after them.

I found myself on the street. I noticed the air was clean, free of soot. It felt pleasant to breathe. It was crowded. I was especially struck by the number of men, without crutches, without wooden legs, and elegantly dressed to boot. The women were wearing beautiful coats, sometimes furs. I couldn't see any padded or quilted work jackets. The faces seemed calm, clean. No fear lurked in their eyes. They talked among themselves on the street, sometimes I could make out someone's loud laugh. Rows of beautiful apartment houses stretched along the streets. Nowhere were there any traces of ruins or walls standing suspended in air. I saw a Catholic church straight ahead. It was Sunday. There was no service taking place, but many people were praying. They were also well dressed and looked prosperous. In the choir, a nun was singing in a beautiful, clear voice.

I reported to the address I'd been given in the dean's office. Everything went completely smoothly. They didn't ask for any identification or any other documents. The woman working there just wrote down my name; she ordered another employee to take me to the dormitory. It turned out to be a beautiful apartment house, abandoned by its inhabitants as they departed the area that the Soviet Union had captured. My guide took me to a spacious apartment with three rooms. She suggested I take the last one, since the first two were connecting rooms. Two students were already living in there, so I took the third bed. As soon as I was alone—and my guide warmly said goodbye—I started taking a look around. In amazement and disbelief I touched the white, clean walls and floors, which didn't even have gaps between the boards. What gave me the greatest thrill were the three large windows with whole, clean panes and frames painted white. They opened and closed easily. Once I'd enjoyed the windows to their fullest, I set about testing the bed. The beautifully shining, nickel-plated rails were eye-catching; I found the webbing under the mattress extraordinary: it was woven so thickly that you couldn't even see any gaps. The mattress turned out to be phenomenal; there were sheets, a pillow, and a quilt. I rolled back and forth with joy on the bed and it was still hard for me to believe that everything was really here and that I was here—for real, not in my dreams.

The fact no one had checked my documents, that someone had sent me here on purpose, the wonderful conditions I'd found here—it was all cause for incredible joy.

If this is how Chernivtsi is, and this is how Bukovina is, I thought, *imagine how Poland must be!* The dream of Poland, where everyone could live the way they wished and where they wished, where there was no need to fear for your life, where there was no exile and there had never been either the GPU or the NKVD, where no one informed on anyone else because all were brothers—the dream that so many Polish families in Ukraine had—became closer to me here than anywhere before.

After a few days, classes began. Lectures were held in a large hall furnished on one side with pharmacy cabinets and full of chairs for the students. Except there was considerable confusion among the professors and teaching assistants. The locals couldn't bear the newly arrived Russian staff, who—naturally—had been granted all the top jobs. The anatomy professor didn't want to, and maybe couldn't, lecture in Russian; he spoke Ukrainian. The locals were leaving with increasing frequency.

Chernivtsi: Red Army soldiers enter the city.

In Chernivtsi I got word that my younger brother, Lucjan, had died.

I knew from letters that he'd been badly wounded and spent a long time in a hospital in Smolensk. He fell in love with a nurse, who helped him stay there longer. She clearly reciprocated his feelings, because she soon fell pregnant. Lucjan dreamed of getting leave for R&R at his parents' house in Chernigovka. But it didn't work out that way. Shortly after being discharged from the hospital, he ended up back on the front lines. He often sent short letters: *As long as I'm alive, I'll write.* Sometimes somewhere in the corner he would add in tiny letters: *I'm suffering hunger and cold.* His last letter was dated April 5, 1945: *We're constantly in heavy fighting, very many of us are being killed. Tomorrow there'll be an offensive on a large city.* (It was forbidden to mention names in letters.) *If I survive, I'll write.*

He didn't write. After a while my parents in Chernigovka received a so-called "pokhoronka." It read that my brother had died honorably on April 7, 1945. He fell at Berlin.

It would have been impossible to get to Smolensk to track down my would-be sister-in-law. I don't know and never will whether Lucjan had a son or a daughter, or whether mother and child survived.

The end of the sixth semester was approaching. All the free time I had left I dedicated to walking around the city, so that as I wandered I could overhear what people were saying about repatriation.

Everyone who lived in Romania or Poland before the war could emigrate to their own countries. They could also stay and—as it was known in official language—"benefit from the privileges of the Soviet nation." People didn't know what to do, they vacillated.

"Leave everything, my life's work, my home, my land?" said some. Others replied: "Stay and benefit from the privileges of the Soviet nation, of which the most certain is life among the polar bears? No. I've got to leave everything and get out. Get out while I still can."

Few knew these "privileges" better than I did. Yet in my case there was a basic difficulty, for we had lived not within the newly fixed borders of the Polish state, but outside them. We had always lived there, for generations, and it had been Poland for a very, very long time, though only until 1793. The fact we were barely a dozen kilometers from the border with Poland helped little—instead it might do harm.

Yet I had to try.

I started by taking walks down the street where the repatriation office stood. I observed the people who gathered there. I often saw them leaving upset, complaining that a huge number of different documents and certificates had been demanded of them—ones they often didn't have. After some time it occurred to me I could go into the yard and listen to what the applicants standing in little clusters were talking about. It turned out they were loudly criticizing the officials, particularly one Soviet major who was constantly by the side of the Polish commissioner. A woman in a white blouse was disparaging him out loud. I quickly took to my heels, thinking that any moment the police would turn up and arrest not just her, but also anyone so bold as to listen to her.

Before long, I noticed the NKVD officer guarding the entrance fairly frequently left his post. I took advantage of one of those moments to go into the waiting room. This greatly expanded my stock of information. I learned that if someone's case was somewhat uncertain, under no circumstances should they go into the office when that major was there. It made much more sense to wait until the Polish commissioner was there on his own. But that wasn't easy. Even after hours of work, they would leave together and walk off in the same direction. Sometimes the commissioner would turn up in the courtyard; then a little crowd of inquirers would pack around him and bombard him with questions.

Finally a moment came that I decided to seize. I stopped the commissioner right at the entrance to the bathroom.

"Sir, could you please take half a minute to speak to me?"

He stopped expectantly. In a single breath I explained to him where I'd been until 1939.

"I'm Polish, my parents are Polish, and I want to go to Poland," I declared with a passion as great as my dream of emigrating to unknown, yearned-for Poland.

The officer stepped away from the bathroom door.

"You've got parents?" he asked, taking a familiar tone. "Where are they now?"

"In Kazakhstan, we got deported in '36."

"Who have you got in Poland?"

"No one."

"And you want to go there ...?"

"Very badly."

"Do you know everything in Poland is very expensive? Keep thinking about it."

A few days went by. I started hunting for the officer again. This time he noticed me himself.

"I've thought everything through," I said. "I want to go. But I'm afraid of getting arrested and sent back to Kazakhstan. My brother has been in a camp near Magadan since '38, the other was killed at the front. He was drafted into the Red Army and killed at Berlin. On April 7, sir!"

"Brothers by blood?"

"By blood," I confirmed.

After some thought, he replied: "Your papers won't go through in Chernivtsi. You've got to try somewhere in the countryside. There it'll be easier to get a repatriation card."

The academic year was coming to an end. Over the summer we had a month of mandatory practice. I cautiously worked out which villages had repatriation centers. I asked the dean's office to assign me to the village of Panka in Storozhynets Raion. In so doing I earned nothing but pity from my classmates, who couldn't understand—nor were they supposed to—why I was choosing a godforsaken village when there were better places.

In the beginning I started my practice in Panka with a cool head. In the course of a day I usually vaccinated several children against smallpox, gave a couple shots, sometimes I had to bandage someone or give them pills for a headache—in short, it was a piece of cake. Now and then a patient would leave me a couple rubles. If anyone had a fever or lived far away and couldn't come to the clinic, I was happy to visit them at home. I didn't resent spending time on friendly conversation with the women I'd treated. I quickly got to know the community. I earned the villagers' sympathy, which allowed me to gain patients—a greater number than one might expect in such a small town. I became—it's uncouth to say this, but it was true—a popular person. Popular in this neither-town-nor-village—a place that was really Romanian, but had become, unfortunately, Soviet. I lived with a Romanian woman whose husband, a Pole, hadn't yet returned from the military, and she didn't intend to leave for Poland on her own.

After a while I got in touch with the Polish repatriation commissioner. Sure enough, in the countryside it was easier to talk to him one-on-one, away from the presence of his Soviet colleague, or rather, minder. He came to Panka two days a week, and on the other days he served other villages. He repeatedly emphasized that the Soviet government really had agreed to repatriate Poles, but only those who'd lived on Polish territory until 1939. The remainder had no right to repatriation. Apart from that he told me Poland had been heavily damaged during the war. There were no apartments there, it was hard to get food, everything was expensive. Nothing but trouble. I didn't even have relatives over the new border, and it was unlikely I'd manage on my own. Here in Bukovina it was much better, safer.

I helped my Romanian woman at home and in the garden, which made her very happy. After a couple weeks she told me I didn't have to pay her for accommodation; in those days the savings meant a lot to me.

Her mother lived in a little house next door; she was a kind, calm woman, and after work she liked to sit and chat. When she wanted to show sympathy, she often repeated: "Săracii, săracii." I ate breakfast and dinner with them. Most often they cooked mămăligă. Into a mixing bowl they'd pour two cups of beautiful yellow cornmeal; one person slowly poured over it more than a liter of hot milk, freshly boiled in a pot, and the other very quickly stirred the batter with a stick. Well-made mămăligă was fluffy, crunchy, and didn't stick in your mouth. After mixing, they dumped it out of the bowl onto a plate and it looked like egg-yolk babka—you could slice it with a knife and eat it, though most often it was cut into cubes and doused with more hot milk. At the time I thought this made a really delicious dish. There we ate mămăligă mornings and evenings, and bread, much less.

The commissioner finally started talking to me about concrete details. He advised me, above all, to try my best to get a certificate from the mayor saying I was a permanent resident of Panka.

Then I was supposed to find people who would agree to add me to their repatriation card as a member of their family. I should use my own name, since, after all, a sister or female cousin might have a different last name. This really frightened me: since everyone in the village knew one another, someone might do me harm, even inadvertently. Yet we worked out a different, realistic solution. I had to find a family that wasn't leaving, even though they had the right to. The directive provided that if a person who was of age desired at the last minute to stay in the Soviet Union, to—for instance—"continue enjoying the privileges of the Soviet nation," then they would be crossed off the card, which would stay valid for the remaining members of the family. As I've already mentioned, my hostess was not emigrating to Poland, but she could take a card and then withdraw from repatriation.

Evacuation card to Poland from the village of
Panka in Bukovina: the name of Fryzyna Klusek is
crossed out and the author's name added below.

I started trying to discreetly query my patients
about the mayor. It turned out he liked drinking
and had a weakness for women. Someone told me
that not long ago his wife had thrown a giant fit on
the street at his latest woman of choice. She wanted

the woman to give back her horbatka—a striped, hand-woven wool apron—which the mayor had clearly presented to his lover. And this lover was none other than—my hostess!

Birth certificate in Latin, issued to the author by the priest of the Roman Catholic parish in Storozhynets in Bukovina. As a valid document it was meant to ease the formalities in Poland.

So I turned to her for help. I suggested she invite the mayor to dinner, which she was glad to do—and the mayor gave me a certificate!

The document thus acquired, the officer could on that basis without hindrance issue me an evacuation card, on which the name Fryzyna Klusek—as my benefactress was called—had been crossed out, leaving only mine.

I was thrilled. I had my own travel document and I wasn't dependent on anyone. The commissioner said I had to wait for the repatriation train that would be provided for this village. The repatriates had the right to take all their possessions and livestock with them. The departure was planned for October or November.

One Sunday I found myself in conversation with the priest from Starozhynets, boasting that I now had the necessary evacuation documents, and I was leaving for Poland. He replied:

"In Poland the most important document is a birth certificate. Do you have one?"

I didn't.

He told me to come after services to his office, where he gave me a certificate based on the information I supplied him.

"I'm sure it will prove useful," he kept saying.

At the institute in Chernivtsi I asked for my documents, telling them, just in case, that I intended to move to Voronezh, where my parents lived. They were issued to me without any problems.

TO POLAND

Before leaving for Poland, I badly wanted to see Marachivka again, to visit my aunt Maria, who I'd lived with during the Great Famine in 1933. I decided to go there.

I didn't find my aunt at home; she had just gone to Slavuta for Mass. During the occupation, the Germans had reopened the Catholic Church and it was still active—I just didn't know for how much longer. My cousin Hania received me warmly. She brought out everything she had from the pantry: wiśniówka, preserves, she scrambled some eggs. Then my aunt arrived; she was very happy and there was no end to our conversations. She told me how the NKVD had taken away her husband.

"The thing I regret most about all this," she said, "is that the day before, I argued with Antoni. We hadn't had time to make up by the time they came in the night and took him away. I didn't give him anything, not a clean change of underwear or a piece of bread. I always kept a change of underwear ready, but that time I'd washed them, I don't know why, and I was out of bread. They started pounding on the door and took him as he was standing there. I feel miserable that we didn't make up. Along with him, they took his brother Stanisław from Noha-chivka. Stanisław is apparently alive, he was writing from a camp somewhere in the Far East. Someone said Antoni died shortly afterward in prison, still in Slavuta, before they could ship him out like the others. I don't know how he died. They didn't tell me anything. I didn't receive notification. If only they'd at least give his body back, so I could bury it …

УПРАВЛЕНИЕ КОМИТЕТА ГОСУДАРСТВЕННОЙ БЕЗОПАСНОСТИ
УКРАИНСКОЙ ССР

по Хмельницкой области

декабря 1990 г.№ В - 81   281070

На №_____ от _____   Хмельницкая область, г. Славута,
                               ул. Ленина, 33/6
                               Васьковской Е. А.

Уважаемая Евфросиния Антоновна!

На заявление, поступившие из Хмельницкого облисполкома, сообщаем, что Ваш отец - Васьковский Антон Петрович, 1894 года рождения, арестован 28 декабря 1937 г. бывшим Берездовским РО НКВД и необоснованно обвинен в том, что якобы "проводил контрреволюционную националистическую пропаганду". По этому сфабрикованному обвинению 8 февраля 1938 г. комиссар внутренних дел СССР и прокурор СССР приговорили его к расстрелу, который приведен в исполнение 14 марта того же года. Захоронен в братской могиле на старом каменец-подольском городском кладбище (район завода "Электроприбор"), где в 1989 году установлен обелиск памяти жертвам репрессий.

Повторное расследование, проведенное сотрудниками УКГБ по Хмельницкой области, показало полную невиновность Вашего отца, уважаемая Евфросиния Антоновна, и он был посмертно реабилитирован, о чем высылаем копию справки.

К сожалению, это все, что нам известно о трагической судьбе Вашего отца, ставшего жертвой сталинского террора.

Согласно постановлению Совета Министров СССР № 1655 от 8 сентября 1955 г. Вы имеете право получить два месячных оклада по последнему месту работы отца. Для этого необходимо предъявить копии свидетельства о его смерти и справки о реабилитации. Свидетельство о смерти Вы получите в Славутском отделе ЗАГС по извещению, которое мы Вам высылаем.

С глубоким уважением

Сотрудник Управления КГБ   И. Кабачинский

Типография изд-ва. «Поділля». Зак. 3973—20 т. 1985 г.

Letter "rehabilitating" Antoni Waśkowski, shot by the NKVD in 1938 in Kamianets-Podilskyi for alleged subversive activity. In 1990 the new local administration offered compensation to his daughter: her father's final two salary payments. In his case that would be a couple poods of grain.

The next day, Hania and I went to see my family home.

After ten years, the village had changed unrecognizably. Everywhere was black and dirty. The roads, formerly overgrown with thick grass and knotweed, were now churned up by tractors, the ditches destroyed and filled in. Every dozen or so meters, there were deep, mighty puddles full of creamy black mud. A wagon rolled up, loaded with freshly mowed grass. A young boy was driving it. He urged the horses on and struggled through. The horses splashed around up to their bellies, and the driver got splashed too, so, swearing, he wiped his hands off on his pants. But this didn't bother anyone. No one took care to dry the puddle out somehow, to dig new ditches.

"Who cares, the rain'll stop, it'll dry up ..."

We reached the front of the house. The orchard, of which my father had been so proud, had gone wild. I remembered helping my parents plant the saplings. My mother kept saying that if children help plant, the orchard starts bearing fruit faster, the trees become more beautiful, and the fruit tastier. Not even a trace of the fence remained.

The house had two entrances: from the front and from the yard. Through the yard entrance lived Grześko the farmer and his family, and in the more presentable part, in the front, the kolkhoz had placed a very dangerous breeding bull. Everyone was afraid of him; a policeman was meant to come and shoot the animal, but in the meantime over a couple weeks the bull had dug a huge pit there. Finally, Grześko's wife emerged. She invited us into the kitchen, offered us something, and explained where the holes in the wall had come from.

Our neighbor, Sadowska, also came over, having

found out about my arrival. She very warmly invited me over to her house; I didn't want to go and politely declined, but she wouldn't be brushed off and I finally gave in. Her house was very tidy, freshly renovated, clean everywhere; she was very proud of it. She kept showing me what they'd done, what additions they'd built; she bragged that her son worked as an accountant at the kolkhoz and his wife was a teacher, so they were doing comfortably now. She set the table and served me dinner, asking if my parents would return to Marachivka once they were allowed to, although truth be told—she kept saying—there was nothing to return to. Everyone knew Grześko's wife was a lazy housekeeper, everything had gone to pot, rain poured through the hole in the roof onto the cow, but they didn't repair it, everything was falling apart.

Those were her neighborly stories, this was how my childhood home looked now.

I only told my aunt that I intended to emigrate to Poland. For the road, she roasted me a large chicken she'd borrowed from her sister, put some butter in a jar, heavily salted so it wouldn't spoil, added a few jars of preserves, and said:

"God be with you."

When I got back to Panka, the expectant waiting started. I felt time stretching on and on. The academic year began, but I sat there twiddling my thumbs. My further studies, even if I was lucky enough to make it to Poland, were deeply in doubt.

Finally in December the train was provided. People unhurriedly loaded up their possessions.

While practicing in Panka, I'd earned three hundred rubles. It was in small bills, which were also very worn. I exchanged them in a store for new, larger ones. Then I went to the commissioner to thank him for what he'd done for me. I wanted to give him two hundred rubles. He looked at me and smiled warmly:

"My child, how could I take money from you?"

I have to say that inside I was very glad, because although it wasn't a large amount, in my situation every kopeck counted.

Finally the train set off, without particular haste. We often stopped for long periods, to feed the cattle. We crossed the border without any problem. I couldn't believe it.

Here I was in Poland! Incredible!

I kept disembarking at the stations to see what Poland was like.

I saw a kiosk on the platform. The counter, piled with newspapers, also held soap. I bought a square, looked it over, sniffed it, then went back and asked for another. I paid and immediately thought: *Maybe I should try to buy one more?*

"Ma'am, would you sell me another soap?" I asked the clerk.

"Yes, of course, as many as you want."

My whole life soap had been hard to get, and when at times we'd managed to buy some, it was no more than half a piece, or even a quarter. But here, "skol'ko ugodno"—as much as you liked.

At the next station I saw ham sandwiches. I could tell the war had been hard, some cities here were apparently as destroyed as back across the border, but people had something to eat, ham, kiełbasa ...

The train moved very slowly, often stopping, not least because no one knew where it was meant to go—to Pomerania or to Legnica province. Probably wherever there was still fallow land from abandoned German farms. Because after all, these people, the repatriates, had left behind their own land and their own farms back in Bessarabia. No wonder they now expected something in Poland more or less equivalent or even better. But for my part, I had nothing, so I wouldn't get anything either.

I disembarked at one of the stations and went to the ticket counter. I asked what documents were needed to buy a ticket, for instance to Poznań. The ticket seller gave me a surprised look and said that for that I needed money, not documents. I told her I knew I needed money, but apart from that did I also need some kind of pass or komandirovka ... Now impatient, she replied that as long as I paid, I could go where I wanted!

So then I got off, at random, in the town of Konotop, near Zielona Góra.

I walked around the streets a little. I saw little pieces of paper on the doors of houses: *House occupied by X.* I heard some men passing by say:

"The Poznaniaks have already looted everything."

The freedom to travel lured me back to the station. The next stop was called Bojadła. I got off there and walked to the village. I thought that someone in the State Repatriation Office would tell me what I was supposed to do, but they had no branch there at all. The nearest one was located in Zielona Góra.

I looked for a place to spend the night. People I met on the street advised me to go into any house I liked. When I explained that I had no assignment or permission, they replied that everyone was doing it.

"Go right on in, across the street here's an empty house, it's very big, but maybe your parents will come here and you'll live there together."

When someone arrived right after the war and took over a house freshly abandoned by Germans, it sometimes happened that they would pull still-warm bread from the stove, and rows of jellies and preserves would be standing in the basement. The "Poznaniaks" had already taken the best farms, and to us "Lwowiaks," repatriates from the East, now went only the poorer ones.

There were few Germans, the indigenous people, in the village. They went around in black armbands.

I went into the indicated house. Everything was opened up and scattered everywhere, a pile of old shoes lay on the floor, some mattresses were in a corner, bedspreads were on the bed. In the kitchen there were plates and mugs, in the yard, beautifully stacked firewood.

I lit the kitchen stove, swept up, heated some water, washed myself with my freshly bought soap and lay down to sleep. I was awakened by a racket.

It sounded like someone was walking around upstairs; doors and windows were slamming, the wind was howling, and it was raining. I was scared, I thought ghosts were making mischief, that something awful was going on, God knew what. The night stretched on to eternity.

When dawn finally started breaking, I went upstairs

to see what had been going on. There was no trace of ghosts—it had been the wind tearing at the open windows. I closed all the ones I could and went back downstairs.

Then I went to the township building, hoping to get a job. An older man, the township secretary, put my name in his notebook and said they had no job for a feldsher, but they needed a midwife.

Very well, I would be a midwife. Equipped with gauze and scissors for cutting umbilical cords, I headed off to my first labor, in the house of a repatriate family from near Lviv. They had taken over the better part of the house; on the other side lived a German man who hadn't emigrated. I heard the husband of the birthing woman say to the German:

"Don't go to bed, we might have to go get a doctor, prepare the horses."

If I remember right, the young mother was named Agata Sznycel; it was a quick labor, with no complications. The newborn's father drank a lot at the birth celebration and only late that night did he remember the German wasn't asleep and was still waiting at the ready. I saw him sitting in his cap with a crop in hand, prepared for the road. When he was told the child had been born and a doctor wasn't needed, he went out to the stable to check on the horse.

But the births after that included some difficult cases. The mayor's wife went into labor. For a long time the placenta wouldn't separate and the umbilical cord wouldn't lengthen. I didn't think it seemed like placenta accreta, but the mother was very delicate, so I started fearing for how things might go. I advised the baby's father to try and get a doctor. The mayor fairly quickly brought a doctor from the neighboring village, and she soon expelled the placenta using Credé's maneuver. After the birth, the mayor's wife took it easy for a long while; for two weeks she didn't want to get out of bed. The whole time I kept coming to see her, washing her, changing the bedsheets, bathing the baby, helping with some housework. Finally I told her to get up and start walking around. She rose, walked a little, and claimed she felt weak. The next day, as if out of spite, phlebitis developed in her left leg. A swollen leg, considerable pain, a high fever. This time the mayor's wife really was sick. It took a few weeks for all the symptoms to recede and the patient fortunately to recover.

Often in the area, the local "grandmothers" helped women in labor, and I was only called in for complicated births, when an obstetrician and a hospital were needed.

I remember that once I was asked to come see a woman in labor who I found in overall terrible condition: a stillbirth, in transverse position, a little macerated arm even hanging out of her vagina. I transported the woman on an ordinary wagon to the hospital in Nowa Sól, and the labor ended with the fetus being dissected.

The next case was a primigravid woman already advanced in years; she was forty. The woman gave birth to a large baby, but the placenta was ingrown and she started bleeding. There was no doctor nearby. A nun arrived, but she had no idea how to manually remove a placenta, and the birthing mother was still bleeding, growing paler and weaker. Her eyes were going dark. I gave her an injection of glucose with vitamin C. The priest came for extreme unction, but the doctor still hadn't arrived. Over the phone he and I had arranged that he'd drive his own car to the Odra River, and on the other side, a wagon would be waiting. But there was an issue with the crossing. It was spring of 1946. The Odra was rough, ice floes were growing dangerously tall and floating densely on the high water. All that ensured the crossing was a small ferry operated by one man, who knew his task well, but this time was understandably frightened. He refused, and there was no bridge nearby. Finally the ferryman was persuaded—not for free. The ferry went across and the doctor manually removed the placenta on the spot. The mother stopped bleeding. The doctor also left us a few tablets of Prantozil in case of infection and suggested that—if septicemia, meaning blood infection, developed—I absolutely call him and he would help organize transportation to the hospital.

I was truly amazed when I heard him demand five thousand złotys from the mother's husband for the procedure. Of that, he counted out a thousand and gave it to me. I refused it, but he was firm and kept saying he always paid his assistants. He encouraged me to come to Zielona Góra, where I'd be able to learn obstetrics at the hospital.

The patient quickly returned to health and luckily no infection occurred. Every day she was given very filling chicken soup, in the place of a blood transfusion.

Following the doctor's advice, I went to Zielona

Góra. Yet the county doctor had no particular desire to talk; he demanded many different documents, authenticated by a sworn translator. I didn't really know where to find such a person, nor did I have the money for one.

Sometimes I was asked how much I was owed for assisting a birth, but I never dared to name a figure; finally the interested parties would conclude I was obviously paid by the township or the health insurance fund, while in reality I had no salary at all.

Back in the Soviet Union, no one had taught me that a person should be paid for work and that you had to demand it. The meager pennies we sometimes got didn't really bear any relation to the work we performed.

I was sure of one thing: I shouldn't stay in the countryside any longer, left to nothing but my own strengths and skills. I concluded I had to get into a hospital.

I got on a train heading southwest. At first I intended to go to Jelenia Góra, but what was the harm in going further? Finally I decided on Lubań, which wasn't so far from the German border.

I tracked down the city hospital. I took a seat in the lobby among the people waiting. A very sonorous male voice was coming from the first floor. Someone was horribly berating someone else, Russian curse words were piling up, and the filthiest ones at that, "pyatietazhnye."[20] I struck up a conversation with my neighbor. He explained to me we

20 "Five-story" ones, i.e. very crude.

were clearly hearing Doctor Komendziński, who was German, but had learned Russian at the front. Other people also joined the conversation. Everyone unanimously praised the doctor, saying what a wonderful surgeon he was, a specialist in abdominal procedures and limb amputations; they said he could skillfully remove a thyroid, perform skin grafts following trophic ulcers and burns, and so on. I also learned that the surgical and obstetrics and gynecology ward was located upstairs, while the ground floor held internal medicine and the venereal disease ward, both run by Pani Komendzińska, who was also a doctor. Both he and she—just the two of them—did all this work, despite the fact that there was also a county doctor, Doctor Wancy, but he was rarely seen around there.

By the time I stood before Doctor Komendziński I knew a great deal about the hospital. I said I was looking for a job, I had graduated from feldsher-midwifery school and I had three years of study at Medical Institutes under my belt: in Alma-Ata, in Kharkiv, and finally in Chernivtsi. The doctor's response was brief:

"That is a lot and nothing. I need nurses. Stay, I'll see what you know how to do."

That very day I started working on the surgical ward. It held many war invalids, mainly young and in grave health. One of them was named Wiśniewski, he had been repeatedly wounded, and besides that was beset with various complications. He had a perirenal abscess, he was very thin and feverish. There was a German nun he wouldn't let near him. Once he kicked her so hard in the stomach that she flew over two beds. No wonder the German woman gave his ward a wide berth. She and I worked together, but she left me completely in charge of caring for Wiśniewski. Apart from him, there were another seven young soldiers on that ward. They were very kind and treated me irreproachably. Those who could walk helped me change the sheets of the ones who were seriously ill, and even assisted with procedures.

There was a lot of work, from early morning to the late evening hours. I was given a room furnished with a bed and sheets, a table and a cabinet. The bathroom was right next door, in the hallway. I had never lived in such luxurious conditions. I would eat in the cafeteria, three meals a day; the food was very good and aesthetically served: a table covered with a white tablecloth, porcelain and proper silverware, the soup in a tureen, the main course on platters. The hospital secretary and the nurses from Poznań province would whine really foolishly and audaciously—this was too fatty, that was too tough, or didn't taste good, but I, and another two women apart from me, a mother and daughter, ate everything up with relish.

Pani Ćwiertniewska worked as an midwife, and her daughter Marysia was my age. They both lived at the hospital like I did, and we quickly struck up a true friendship. They came from Višnieva, near Lida in what is now Belarus. After the Soviet invasion in 1939, the NKVD arrested Pan Ćwiertniewski, who had been a well-known feldsher in that area. His wife and two children, Marysia and Czesio, were deported to Siberia. Czesio made it to the West with

Anders' Army, while his mother and sister made it back to Poland, admittedly not to their home region, which had been lost to the Soviet Union, but to the so-called Recovered Territories in the west.

After a few days of work, the nun reported on my skills to Doctor Komendziński. He asked me into his office and told me the situation the hospital was in. Two young orderlies—former German officers who were assisting with operations, moving patients, making dressings and casts—were returning to Germany. Fräulein Schade, a third-year medical student, the third person with training at the hospital, was also leaving. Doctor Komendziński alone would remain and had already applied for Polish citizenship; his grandfather was Polish. Finally, he said:

"Maybe you'll be able to replace Fräulein Schade. Follow her everywhere for a few days, from morning to evening, watch her performing her assigned treatments, observe what is kept where, how to prepare fluid for ivs, and so on. Don't count on her explaining anything to you because, firstly, she doesn't speak Polish, and, secondly, she hates Poles so much that she doesn't talk to them at all."

Back then there were no premixed fluids, such as glucose or normal saline. Nor was there disposable equipment for ivs or blood transfusions. There were no disposable syringes. You had to prepare 5, 10, and 40 percent saline and glucose in glass flasks. In the same way, we would sterilize cow's milk for intramuscular injections for women with chronic oophoritis, as part of immunostimulation therapy.

We heard a lot of good things about penicillin, but

few patients with lobar pneumonia had access to this wonderful drug. It did happen that a patient's family would get a package from abroad with crystalline penicillin. It was administered every three hours, in doses of only 30,000 units, but its effect was really extraordinary: a patient with severe pneumonia, unable to get out of bed under his own strength for two weeks, with high fever, pain including stabbing pain in the chest, and a pestering cough, treated to no avail with compresses, cupping-glasses, aspirin, camphor—after a few injections of penicillin, by the second day would have a reduced temperature, be able to sit up in bed himself, and be rapidly returning to health.

I followed Fräulein Schade in lockstep for two days—just as Doctor Komendziński had ordered. I observed her and did my best to memorize everything. Sure enough, she didn't speak a word to me. She was fierce and self-contained. I didn't get to know her better, because she left on the third day. But I took her place and felt this could be a great opportunity for me.

Doctor Komendziński started work at five in the morning. At that hour he felt fresh and rested, and in summer it was still cool. I'd arrive half an hour earlier, to give the first surgery patient Avertin, an intrarectal anesthesia. The day before, the doctor would always assign three morning operations. The hardest procedures would go at first light: gastric resection, removing gallstones, or removing the thyroid. Secondly he would operate on hernias and perform appendectomies. After finishing work, he would say happily:

"It's eight o'clock, and all the scheduled operations are done."

Seeing he was in a good mood, I would joke that if he started at two in the morning he could eat his breakfast by five.

From the operating room, after changing his apron, he'd go to his office, where his first meal would be brought to him from home: a pot of chicory coffee with milk, rolls and soft-boiled eggs or lunchmeat. The pot was covered with a cozy so that the coffee didn't get cold. After breakfast he would go on his rounds, scheduling operations for the next day and giving orders. He would check to make sure I'd gotten everything written down. After an appointment came dressings, then often an operation again: acute appendicitis, an incarcerated hernia, a caesarean section or a forceps birth. The doctor and his family lived right next to the hospital. If necessary, no matter the time of day or night, he would immediately stand ready to operate.

I remember once, after an explosion in a boiler room, we received some badly wounded people with extensive second- and third-degree burns. In this case we immediately put the patients under using ether, to bring them out of shock, and on the dressing table we washed their wounds with warm water and soap, removing the coal, rags, and soot; at the same time we wiped away the flakes of burned skin. Next, the injured surface and the whole skin was bathed with 70 percent rectified spirit, after which the patient was transferred to sterile bedsheets, under a so-called hood with light bulbs, to warm up the body. It was a draconian method, but we got good results.

The way blood transfusions took place was with the donor and recipient lying next to one another on two tables, and the surgeon standing in the middle, continually giving blood to the recipient with a syringe. If there was a donor with the same blood type at hand, good, if not, they were given group O. At that time we didn't yet test for Rh and there were no blood donation centers.

At noon, the doctor went home to rest, and Pani Komendzińska would stay a long time at the hospital. In the morning she assisted her husband on operations, and then she performed various procedures herself. Many women were brought in with blood loss from miscarriages—spontaneous or artificially induced. There was not yet a law on terminating a pregnancy. Every bleeding woman needed to have her uterus curetted. After sorting out the most urgent cases, the doctor would take appointments in the VD, TB, and internal medicine wards.

We gave syphilis patients Salvarsan twice a week intravenously and bismuth intramuscularly. Patients with pulmonary TB mainly got calcium or glucose intravenously. As I've mentioned, there were no disposable needles. We had to keep boiling and sharpening them. And also applying cupping glasses, compresses, and many other activities ... To get it all done, I'd be buzzing around from morning to night.

I remember Doctor Komendziński and Doctor Komendzińska very well and I truly owe them a great deal. I learned how to assist in an operation, administer an anesthetic drip, manually expel a placenta, perform uterine curettage, put a cast on a broken bone without displacement, and so on.

The couple had two preschool-aged children who lived with Doctor Komendzińska's parents and sister. Her father was a Protestant minister and he, his wife and younger daughter soon left for Germany, while the doctors stayed in Lubań. If I remember right, Poles at the time earned an average of 3,000 złotys a month, but Doctor Komendziński, who was native to the region, earned. . . 190 złotys. That was enough for two kilos of tomatoes (but this was back before the currency change). The Komendzińskis lived off of the fees their patients paid.

Sometimes they invited me over. The doctor would complain that he had nothing to operate with, his tools kept breaking, there was no anesthetic or surgical thread. He couldn't refuse to help his patients, but how could he operate here if he had no way to sew up an abdomen? Medical equipment could be bought in Germany, where food, on the other hand, was short. The Komendzińskis therefore planned an excursion across the German border and suggested I join them. I was happy to accept, though it didn't occur to me that there was a certain risk associated with it.

We went in an ambulance. The doctor drove, his wife sat in the back with a backpack loaded with lunchmeat, and I was in the passenger's seat, next to the driver. If the border guards stopped us, we were meant to say we were driving to see someone seriously ill. The doctor, who knew the area well, kept telling me the names of the local villages. Luckily we got to the Nysa River without incident. Pani

Komendzińska took her backpack and forded the river. The man we had arranged to meet appeared on the other side, and they continued on together. The next day in the evening we came to the same spot at an agreed time. Poor Pani Komendzińska was shivering with cold under a tree. It turned out the night before, the clocks had changed from summer time to standard time, and she'd been waiting for us for an hour!

Those months in Lubań were very important for me. The work was thrilling, I didn't have to worry about food or a roof over my head, and I had two close girlfriends.

Once, the hospital received an allocation of food packages from UNRRA. They were heavy, I think they weighed thirty-two kilos apiece. One package was to be shared between two employees. Both Pani Ćwiertniewska and I struggled to drag our package into our room. There was no end of cries of rapture: inside was a can of perhaps 1.5 kilos of sliced pork meat submerged in aromatic lard, affixed with a Russian label: *svinaya tushonka*—I still remember the flavor of that stew, extremely fragrant and delicious. There was a second can with bacon, yet another with frankfurters, and also some kind of sweetly prepared meat, powdered eggs, cigarettes that we could immediately sell off for a good price, napkins for wiping our mouths, and even toilet paper—pink and soft as anything! I thought to myself that in the Soviet Union a mere mortal would have no chance of getting a package like this one.

There were jokes going around on that subject. Roosevelt comes to visit Stalin. After every meal, he thanks him for the tea. Finally someone timidly asks why he's only saying thank you for the tea. Roosevelt replies: "Because everything I've eaten has been my own."

From England, Czesio Ćwiertniewski sent American canned food; sometimes he'd tuck one nylon stocking into an envelope—to reduce the risk of theft—and its mate would usually arrive in the next letter. Back then we wore so-called "gazówki," made of cheap material resembling gauze, but they easily ran and fell apart at the slightest snag. Foreign nylons were something else—super-thin, long, elegant, strong! Untearable. Sometimes I'd properly scrape my calf, but my stocking would be whole! But in those days such a pair of stockings cost six thousand złotys!

I worked in Lubań from May to October 1946.

WROCŁAW

I really wanted to finish my studies.

I made my way to the Medical Academy in Wrocław. The secretary in the dean's office, Pani Żuciadłowa from Lviv, was not an angel in the least. Her name sounded like the Polish word for *bile*, and the students joked she could really pour bile on any inquirers. Her intense dislike of Soviets was widely known, and she immediately counted me among their number. Me! When I asked her to put me down for a conversation with the dean, right away she said there were already forty students on the list, which would take him some two or three weeks, so for now she wasn't accepting further appointments. I wasn't able to win her over completely, though I explained that I'd come from Lubań, I was working, and so on. I could clearly feel her prejudice—an insurmountable obstacle!

Dejected, I went into the waiting room, where the students with appointments for that day were waiting: a few soldiers, along with two elegantly dressed, made-up ladies. I listened to their conversations: one of the girls had been taking secret wartime classes in Warsaw, someone else had done two years of college in Lviv before the war, someone else was joking that if the dean was in a good mood, he'd credit everything.

Suddenly we heard an angry exchange from the office. Someone shouted loudly:

"Five years I fought for Poland!"

Then the door opened and an enraged lieutenant burst out into the waiting room, fulminating against the dean in rather coarse language. He didn't care much that the dean could hear everything. The space in front of the door emptied out, somehow no one was keen to go in now. Then two waiting soldiers suggested that I seize the opportunity right then. I explained that I'd come last and wasn't on the list at all, but they didn't relent and almost forcibly pushed me inside.

Student ID for the University of Wrocław. The medical school at the time was part of the university.

Inside the dean's office, I hadn't even managed to say "hello" before an alarm clock started ringing—an alarm clock I was carrying in my bag! I'd never had a wristwatch; once I asked a man for the time and he thought I was accosting him. Since then, I always went to my most important appointments with a borrowed alarm clock. I started feverishly digging around in my felt drawstring bag, but the cursed alarm clock kept ringing and ringing, and with every passing second I fell deeper into embarrassment! I'd wanted so badly to make a good impression! The dean burst out laughing. He looked over my documents and ... credited me with three years of study in the Soviet Union! But he told me to retake my exams in microbiology and pathological anatomy, and gave me two years to pass a Polish high school diploma exam.

There were around a hundred of us in fourth year, and in fifth, only twenty-five. Some lectures, like internal medicine and neurology, we had jointly with the fifth-years. I had to retake our first pathological anatomy exam; after that I passed all of them. During this time I was working in a hospital in the obstetrics-gynecology department. I mainly had night and holiday shifts, since during the day I was going to lectures and exercises. In my fifth year I got a scholarship and I was no longer permitted to work.

One day Władysław Orłowski tracked me down in Wrocław. We'd known each other since we were kids; the Orłowskis had ridden in the same train car with us to Kazakhstan. At first, exiles—as doubtful, if not hostile elements—weren't drafted into the military at all, but after the German-Soviet war broke out, they took everyone, even women. Władek had been in the Red Army, but managed to get transferred to Berling's First Polish Army. After the war ended, all the soldiers who'd been exiles or came from territories the Soviets had annexed after the First World War wanted to stay in Poland, but Marshal Rokossovsky ordered them to demobilize and return. Władek got married in Poland, which meant he could stay in the Polish Armed Forces.

When we met up, he was heading off on leave to see his parents in Chernigovka and offered himself as a willing emissary to bring a package for my family as well. I was glad and packed up a lot of different clothes, which were what was hardest to get your hands on in Kazakhstan. After he returned, happy his mission had been completed, he came to tell me how his trip had gone:

"Your mother gave me a letter. They say thank you for the package, they were really pleased. No one gave me a hard time at the border, I got everything through! The journey to Taiynsha only took me a week. In '36 we rode for about a month, remember?"

Yet the return journey didn't go so smoothly. He was held at the border under suspicion of being in the collaborationist Vlasov Army. An interrogation and strip-search began. They told him to undress, and meanwhile he didn't even have briefs! He'd left all his personal underwear in Kazakhstan. The investigating officer inspected him carefully, measured his war scars, took pictures. His uniform also got a careful looking-over, and Władek spent many hours in some corner, naked as the day God made him. Finally they let him go. He told me all the news from Chernigovka: who had died, who was alive, how they were getting on. The food was so-so, the clothes were worse, everyone's were tattered and there was no question of buying anything, though the commandant kept promising deliveries of some kind.

In 1948, I received my certificate of completion. Within three years I had to pass another twelve exams for a diploma. But now I could work, with the title and qualification of "acting doctor!" The professors meanwhile suggested not rushing the exams. They made the case it was better to work for a while in a hospital, acquire practical information, and only then take the exams. Apparently before the war it used to take even longer to get a diploma. I was also shaping up for another run-in with bilious Pani Żuciadłowa, who, knowing I was graduating, announced she wouldn't give me a diploma because I didn't have Polish citizenship. In vain I tried to persuade her that neither my grandparents nor my parents had renounced their Polishness. She had made up her mind, and to her I was a citizen of the Soviet Union. Meaning, what can I say—a hated "Sovietka!"

In late August 1948—thanks in part to that fanatic's influence—I applied for recognition of my Polish citizenship and a declaration that I renounced my previous one. After a certain time, the director of the appropriate office told me he was required to inform the secret police of my request; if after a month they had no reservations, a court would look into the matter. Yet I found the time waiting for the security service's decision very difficult. After the experiences I've done my best to describe here, sometimes fear for my own fate and mistrust of those who, illegitimately, could decide it, became overpowering and hard to face down.

At the time I was working in St. Anne's Hospital in Wrocław, which had not yet been nationalized. There was a shortage of doctors, so they employed fourth- and fifth-year medical students. There were few lay nurses. It was the Sisters of Charity who ensured the hospital could function. They worked in every position: the administration, the kitchen, the laundry, and as nurses on the wards. They would start at five in the morning, and end late in the evening. The hospital was sparkling clean, while the patients, bathed and fed, lay on white bedding, hand-sterilized and ironed. The nuns found time for everything and I saw them as a model of hard work.

One day in the hospital office, two gentlemen arrived and said they'd like to see me. One of them I immediately recognized: it was the commissioner who'd helped with my repatriation. He asked me to return my repatriation card. I thought to myself, never in my life will I give it up! I replied calmly that I had destroyed the card after crossing the border. I don't know if he believed me, nor do I know why he wanted to recover the card. Maybe he got in trouble because of me? In any event he told me I'd done the right thing destroying it, because it was invalid now anyway. He also said I would get a government ID that I would use as identification, and no one would give me any trouble.

I never saw him again after that.

After many months of nervous waiting, during which every day I trembled at the thought that instead of getting citizenship I would end up back in Kazakhstan, finally a response came! I received a summons to a court hearing. The result was that my yearned-for citizenship was recognized, and I was issued the appropriate document. This was on December 22, 1949. For me, this was a historic date: the day when I liberated myself from tough, malevolent fears and the weight of them was finally lifted from my mind.

The author as a trainee doctor.

In all this time I was also working at the Ursulines' hospital in Karłowice and in a health center in Tarnogaj. I was living in the hospital building, where I had a lovely, big room. Then I used all my savings to buy an apartment in the town, in an ex-German building. But unfortunately it wasn't a notarized purchase. In those days Poles took empty apartments without being allocated them. The people who sold me the apartment took the compensation and left, leaving behind a few broken pieces of furniture. Yet they hung onto the keys and a few weeks later they reappeared, taking one of the two rooms. They managed to spoil the shared apartment for me, so I quickly moved out—luckily, for good.

On December 11, 1950, I passed my final exam and received my diploma.

Now nothing stood between me and happiness!

On February 1, 1951, I was meant to start a job in Kłodzko. The day before I left, I went to visit the Zarzeckis, a couple I had befriended. We often studied together for our exams. At their place I found a tall and handsome medical student, Florian Michalski, who had come to get some kind of doctor's note for his friends. I wrote up the note for him. We talked about work assignments and exams. It turned out he still had plenty to take, but wasn't too worried about work assignments. A week later he showed up unexpectedly at the hospital in Kłodzko, saying he'd stopped by on his way to visiting his mother, who lived in Kudowa. Another time I ran into him on a train platform and we rode to Wrocław together. On my way back to Kłodzko, I ran into him again at the station, this time in Wrocław. From then on, we met up more often and without any need for excuses. I spent time in Wrocław, yet

Florian more often came to see me in Kłodzko, where I had a lovely two-room apartment with a large kitchen and foyer.

Florian Michalski, the author's fiancé and future husband, after returning from Erlangen.

My fiancé was distinguished by a lively disposition and optimistic view of life; unlike me, he didn't worry about just any old thing.

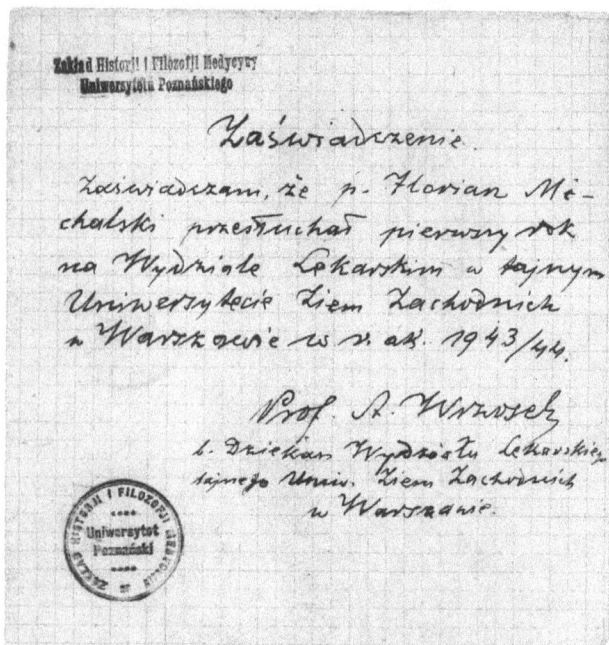

Florian Michalski, being from Wielkopolska, did his first year of medical school at the underground University of the Western Lands, organized in Warsaw during the occupation years by a well-known scholar from Poznań, Professor Adam Wrzosek. This is a declaration that Florian passed his first year.

He came from a wealthy landowning family in the western region of Wielkopolska; their estates, Gorzewo, Nieborza, and Dąbrówka, were seized by the German military in the first days of the war, while all the members of the household were deported to the occupation zone known as the General Government. Florian, born in 1920, ended up in Warsaw; he spent the whole German occupation there. It was during the occupation that he started studying medicine in Warsaw at the underground University of the Western Lands, run by Professor Wrzosek. He was in the Home Army and took part in the Warsaw Uprising; he fought in the Bolt Battalion in the Śródmieście district. After the uprising's defeat, he and many Home Army soldiers were taken out of Warsaw and placed in a POW camp in Moosburg in Bavaria. When the camps were liberated by the American military, he enrolled at the well-known medical school in Erlangen. But after getting word that his mother was gravely ill, he returned to Poland and continued his education in Wrocław.

We both came from families who the whirlwind of history had stripped of literally everything: of the full achievement of generations, of many loved ones, even of a place to live. As a veteran of the Home Army, which was loyal to Poland's prewar government, Florian was required to identify himself. He didn't do so. The secret police were hunting for people like him. They would organize traps that lasted several days in the apartments of previously captured Home Army veterans, into which the prisoners' friends would fall unawares.

We married in 1951. We both wanted badly to get my remaining family out of Kazakhstan and into Poland. Yet all the repatriation offices kept turning us down. This had been my experience too: repatriation didn't apply to Poles who lived on Soviet territory before

1939. We kept going to Warsaw, doing the rounds of various departments, getting vague promises that some legislation was meant to be passed, or were sent away empty-handed. Once at the City Board on Saski Square we were leaving the office of the chairman, who had categorically refused our request. Dejected, we sat down in the hallway, and then an older gentleman who'd noticed us earlier in the lobby approached us; he looked around and said in a quiet voice:

"Head over to the Capital City Council on Nowy Świat and quote the law from 1920, which is still in force."

We ran straight there and to our amazement we were issued the necessary document that we were meant to send to my parents. A kind lady meanwhile suggested we send it as an insured letter, estimating its value at forty Swiss francs, then it would definitely get there. She emphasized that we must put exactly that amount, no more, no less. We did this as well and our invitation reached my parents. The more open political conditions after Stalin's death also eased the emigration procedure. Prisoners were being released from the camps. My brother Władek walked free as well, and arrived at my parents' house in Chernigovka. Right away he began efforts (which included consuming considerable amounts of alcohol with the commandant) to arrange the joint return of my parents and sister to Ukraine.

After a happy return from Kazakhstan to Marachivka, my parents did their best to recover their house. All the villagers supported them. Finally the kolkhoz agreed to sell their home back to them for 1,200 rubles.

COMITÉ INTERNATIONAL DE LA CROIX-ROUGE

AGENCE CENTRALE DE RECHERCHES

Chèques postaux 12-5527
Téléphone 34 60 01
Télégr.: Intercroixrouge
Télex 22 269

Form. I

Rappeler dans la réponse:
DP.124.241/sk

CH - 1211 GENÈVE
7, AVENUE DE LA PAIX

Genève, le 24.8.1976

ATTESTATION

L'Agence centrale de Recherches certifie que selon la documentation qu'elle possède :

Nom, prénoms	MICHALSKI Florian
Date de naissance	4.4.1920
Lieu de naissance	Nieborza
Fils de	--
Grade	soldat
Incorporation	21me rég.d'infanterie A.K.
Matricule	--

a été fait prisonnier le -, des suites de l'insurrection de Varsovie 1944

et interné aux Stalags: 318 et VII-A

sous le numéro 104.094

Le renseignement ci-dessus est attesté par :
carte de présence au Stalag VII-A du 14.11.1944.-

Florian Michalski's post-war documents: a certificate from the Stalag he was sent to as a member of the Home Army (Twenty-First Infantry Division), as well as a transcript with a photo and exams credited at the medical school in Erlangen.

Eigenhändige Unterschrift des Buchinhabers:

Florian Michalski:

Zur Beachtung!

Das Studienbuch gilt für die **gesamte** Studienzeit des Inhabers.

Das **Buch** ist der alleinige Studiennachweis bei der Meldung zu den Prüfungen. Es ist also eine **wichtige Urkunde**, die sorgfältig zu verwahren ist.

Die Ausstellung einer Zweitschrift des Studienbuches ist mit Zeitaufwand und erheblichen Kosten verknüpft.

Nachdruck verboten! Ostdeutsche Druckerei und Verlagsanstalt, Halle (Saale).

My parents came to Poland in April 1955.

In June 1956, after leaving our three young children under their care, my husband and I set off for the Soviet Union. I wanted Florian to meet my whole family. We stayed with my sister in Marachivka. My family was cautioned by a local official that visitors from Poland had to register in Slavuta within twenty-four hours of their arrival. We presented ourselves at the township office. They took away our passports, which we had to come and collect before we left, and we were forbidden from any kind of travel around the country. This didn't surprise us, because since the October Revolution the whole Soviet Union had demonstrated extremely limited hospitality. That was the custom there. That was the landscape. We were to remain in Marachivka, at my family's.

Two days later at three in the morning we heard knocking at the window. It was a neighbor, a Ukrainian man, who was friendly with my parents. Sometimes he managed to pick up Radio Free Europe; a moment before he'd heard that there was a revolution in Poland, and that some people had been wounded and killed in Poznań.

We wanted to get straight back. At the break of dawn we traveled to Slavuta to get our passports, but the chief said he had already sent them to Khmelnytskyi, the oblast capital. With lightning speed, we ordered a phone call home. But the operator replied that the line was busy and would be for the next two weeks. Period. No discussion. Then my brother went into action; he already knew how to negotiate with a chief. After that meeting they both traveled to Khmelnytskyi and brought back the passports. We returned home without any trouble.

In later years contact with Ukraine was easier. We traveled there many times, though I always found the border hugely stressful. Yet we did our best to help our relatives by any possible means and to this day we maintain close contact with them. My brother and sister have passed away, but their children often come to visit us.

This has been the story of my life. I have had a wonderful, brave husband and three successful children, though of those four, only two remain to me. I am glad for my four grandchildren, watching the boys grow into men, and the girls getting more beautiful, while everyone matures more and more fully into the world, which keeps changing ...

I have also worked in the profession that was always my dream. I practice it to this day; at times I have even treated a family through four generations. When my former patients come by, it's impossible for me to turn them down.

I only have difficulty reconciling myself to the past. I still find it inhumane, and at times even not entirely real. Cast out with my loved ones to the depths of degradation, condemned to annihilation or the most difficult bare existence on the deserted steppes, I nonetheless managed to get some education (or at least I started to) and I had a broad, educational practice—and so what if it was often in the most primitive conditions? In a few instances I was granted fate's remarkable favor, which I find no other way of explaining than as an act of Providence, taking me under its wing in a hostile, cruel world. I have also over all these years had amazing, inexplicable luck with people and I still feel deep gratitude toward many of them. Furthermore, I have regained my Homeland, which to me had been always a thing dreamed-for and unknown. I have regained her as one of those unexpected gifts of Providence and I still consider her my most important treasure.

I should be a fulfilled and happy person, yet in fact I am not—if only for the memory of those, my loved ones and others, who remained behind forever.

Siemiatycze, 2005

Translator's Note

Franceska Michalska's memoir tells a remarkable story, one of the many stories of tremendous suffering and hardship faced by Polish people in the twentieth century. As a reader, I am struck by Michalska's matter-of-fact descriptions of events that are by any measure horrific. Her authorial voice, perhaps informed by her experience as a doctor, is plain-speaking, verging on blunt, and completely free of sentimentality or affect. For a translator used to more ornamental literary texts, I wondered whether to soften her rough edges and produce a version that is more polished. But ultimately Michalska's plainspokenness is, I think, a reflection of a person for whom tragedy and suffering were a part of everyday life. I concluded it was important to convey her voice just as she expressed it, and I hope I have succeeded.

Michalska spent much of her life in a multilingual environment, as is reflected in her book. This presents a few challenges for a translator. Many of the cities and towns in this book are known by multiple names in multiple languages, without any one "standard" English form. The same person might refer to Marachivka when speaking Ukrainian and Maraczówka when speaking Polish, with both names being equally valid. The translator into English, however, must choose a single form, while somehow avoiding implying something, inadvertently or otherwise, about a town's "true" identity. In a highly multiethnic region, with a history of shifting borders, contested identities, and imperial conquest, any such implication would be misplaced. I also cannot forget that I am translating this book at a time of conflict in Michalska's home region, with Russia's brutal invasion of Ukraine showing the terrible real-world implications of claims to "true" identity or nationhood.

With these factors in mind, for place names that are presently in Ukraine, in this translation I uniformly use their Ukrainian names. Similarly, I have used indigenous Kazakh place names where applicable, rather than Russified forms, and the Polish names of shared Polish-German geographical features, such as the Odra and Nysa Rivers. I do this in part because these are the names a reader can find most readily on a modern map, but also in a spirit of anti-imperial solidarity with Michalska's struggle for freedom.

Personal identity in Eastern Europe can be no less complex than identity of place, and it is common for individuals to use different forms of their names in different languages. For instance, a man might go by Andrzej when speaking Polish, and Andriy when speaking Ukrainian. In this translation, unless Michalska provided specific guidance about an individual's identity, I have used the Polish forms she herself does.

In general, I have sought to verify transcriptions and spellings of the various additional languages Michalska uses in her text: Ukrainian, Russian, Kazakh, Romanian … Where I was unable, I have made an educated guess, and I hope some other reader will be able to discern her true intention. I would like to thank Dawid Mobolaji for his help translating the medical vocabulary Michalska uses, which was well outside my expertise.

We are now in a moment where the last survivors of the wartime generation are passing away. As they do, the middle of the twentieth century passes from lived experience into collective memory. Accounts like Michalska's allow us, however briefly, to reenter that world and see it through her unwavering eyes. This is the essence of these stories', and this book's, tremendous value.

Sean Gasper Bye
Philadelphia
November 2022

SEAN GASPER BYE's translations of Polish literature have been awarded the EBRD Literature Prize and the Asymptote Close Approximations Prize. He has been a Translator-in-Residence at Princeton University, a National Endowment for the Arts Translation Fellow, and Literature and Humanities Curator at the Polish Cultural Institute New York. He lives in Philadelphia and currently serves as the Interim Executive Director at the American Literary Translators Association.

Book Club Discussion Guides on our website.

World Editions promotes voices from around the globe by publishing books from many different countries and languages in English translation. Through our work, we aim to enhance dialogue between cultures, foster new connections, and open doors which may otherwise have remained closed.

Also available from World Editions:

A Little Annihilation
Anna Janko
Translated by Philip Boehm
"An extraordinarily personal and powerful account
of how the worst wartime atrocities affect ordinary
people." —OLGA TOKARCZUK

Dendrites
Kallia Papadaki
Translated by Karen Emmerich
Winner of the 2017 European Union Prize for Literature

Afterlight
Jaap Robben
Translated by David Doherty
This moving novel gives voice to the silent grief of the
mothers of stillborn children.

Where the Wind Calls Home
Samar Yazbek
Translated by Leri Price
"The potent latest from Yazbek weighs the
consequences of the Syrian civil war. This slim novel
packs a punch." —Publishers Weekly

October Child
Linda Boström Knausgård
Translated by Saskia Vogel
"(Boström Knausgård's) first openly autobiographical
book becomes an act of self-examination powerful
enough to match if not surpass those of her
ex-husband's."—*The Guardian*

On the Design

As book design is an integral part of the reading experience, we would like to acknowledge the work of those who shaped the form in which the story is housed.

Tessa van der Waals (Netherlands) is responsible for the cover design, cover typography, and art direction of all World Editions books. She works in the internationally renowned tradition of Dutch Design. Her bright and powerful visual aesthetic maintains a harmony between image and typography, and captures the unique atmosphere of each book. She works closely with internationally celebrated photographers, artists, and letter designers. Her work has frequently been awarded prizes for Best Dutch Book Design.

The passport photo of Franceska Michalska and the stamp featured on the front cover were scanned from Michalska's passport and provided by the original Polish publisher, Oficyna Literacka Noir sur Blanc. The background image featuring a blank envelope was taken by photographer Dan Cristian Pădureț.

The typeface used for the author's name on the cover is DF Camino, designed by Ko Sliggers. Krakow Sans by Pieter Boddaert was used for the title. As a graphic design student in 1994, Boddaert took a class trip to Krakow and captured street signs displaying unfamiliar letters with his camera. The hand-painted letters had extreme thick-thin contrasts. Krakow Sans, never released commercially, was inspired by these handwritten street signs—all of which have now been replaced.

The cover and interior images have been edited by lithographer Bert van der Horst of BFC Graphics (Netherlands) to increase readability.

Euan Monaghan (United Kingdom) is responsible for the typography and careful interior book design.

The text on the inside covers and the press quotes are set in Circular, designed by Laurenz Brunner (Switzerland) and published by Swiss type foundry Lineto.

All World Editions books are set in the typeface Dolly, specifically designed for book typography. Dolly creates a warm page image perfect for an enjoyable reading experience. This typeface is designed by Underware, a European collective formed by Bas Jacobs (Netherlands), Akiem Helmling (Germany), and Sami Kortemäki (Finland). Underware are also the creators of the World Editions logo, which meets the design requirement that "a strong shape can always be drawn with a toe in the sand."

Printed in the USA
CPSIA information can be obtained
at www.ICGtesting.com
JSHW022002280924
70661JS00006B/7

9 781642 861525